Disability Politics and Theory

Disability Politics and Theory

A.J. Withers

Fernwood Publishing • Halifax & Winnipeg

Editing: Curran Faris
Cover Design: John van der Woude
Printed and bound in Canada by Hignell Book Printing

Published in Canada by Fernwood Publishing
32 Oceanvista Lane
Black Point, Nova Scotia, B0J 1B0
and 748 Broadway Avenue, Winnipeg, Manitoba, R3G 0X3
www.fernwoodpublishing.ca

Fernwood Publishing Company Limited gratefully acknowledges the financial support of the
Government of Canada through the Canada Book Fund and the Canada Council for the Arts, the
Nova Scotia Department of Communities, Culture and Heritage, the Manitoba Department of Culture,
Heritage and Tourism under the Manitoba Publishers Marketing Assistance Program and the Province of
Manitoba, through the Book Publishing Tax Credit, for our publishing program.

Library and Archives Canada Cataloguing in Publication

Withers, A. J., 1979-
Disability politics and theory / A.J. Withers.

Includes bibliographical references and index.
ISBN 978-1-55266-473-5

1. Disability studies. 2. Disabilities.
3. People with disabilities. I. Title.

HV1568.2.W58 2012   362.4   C2011-908398-1

Contents

**This book is dedicated
to Sarah and Amina**

For an accessible, plain language guide to this book, please visit:
<http://fernwoodpublishing.ca/disability/>

Acknowledgments

I have so many people to thank for their help, assistance and support with this book. I owe a great debt to Loree Erickson. You have helped my politics evolve over the decade we have known each other, and you seem to always know when I should be challenged and when I should be comforted, which, at least with respect to me, is an impressive skill. Radical disability theory, too, would not exist without your co-development of it and the many Friday Night Fights and Same Saturdays that it evolved from over the years.

Laura Mac, thank you for your compassion, your support and your loving and quiet approach to disability politics. I am so grateful to have you in my life. You have provided countless amounts of feedback, insight and assistance with this book. You have tolerated my interrupting you all the time to "run something by you," as well as the fact that sometimes I have talked about little else but this book. Thank you for all the times you did the dishes, made me dinner or did any other fabulous housemate/best friend things while I was writing frantically. You have provided me with immeasurable amounts of support in this project, for which I am forever grateful. Also, thanks to Sarah Mangle for helping keep the house together when I was writing, for making me food when I wasn't taking care of myself and for your thoughtful comments. Also, thanks for bringing L.D. into my life.

Thank you to everyone in the Ontario Coalition Against Poverty. I grew up in OCAP and owe a tremendous debt to many of its members (past and present) for their mentorship, support and solidarity. And, specifically, I want to thank Sue Collis, for not only being an incredible teacher and example, but also for having more faith in me than I did myself. This book came out of a conversation that I had with Sue in the car; so, thanks for that conversation and for the ride to Kitchener. Thanks to John Clarke and Gaetan Heroux for putting up with me and providing me with a decade's worth of quiet and respectful guidance. Thanks to Sarah Vance for being such a strong organizer and person and for so eagerly and diligently providing me with feedback and support. And special thanks to Stefanie Gude for being who you are, for always setting an example and for being the one to help with some of the more boring parts of this project. I always appreciate your insight, wisdom and generosity, and you deserve so much more credit than you let yourself have. Also, my deepest appreciation to Shawn Brant — thank you for kicking me in the ass more than once and for being the person I could look to whenever I lost faith.

Extra special thanks to Griffin Epstein for your brilliant and challenging comments and your conversations and company. There have been so many times when I have felt completely stuck, and your encouragement has helped me through. There have been other times when you have said something that made my brain spiral again and again and I couldn't stop writing. Thank you for the important feedback on this entire manuscript, as well as for your help with the many hours of research. Disability organizing in Toronto and the radical disability model would not be what it is today without your important interventions and contributions.

Sean Lee-Popham, it has been a long road and we have been through a lot together; thank you for everything. And thank you Sean, Brian and Connor for providing me (and so many others) with a calm, beautiful space to hide out and hang out in. Geoffrey Reaume, thanks for the challenging and insightful conversations in recent months about disability models. Also, I want to thank you, Mom (Linda Withers), for your support, for your compassion and for picking up on things that I don't always think you will.

To Matt Leitold, thank you for your years of friendship and unwavering support. I know how hard it has been, and you have my gratitude and my admiration. You have been so important in my life, and we both know there were times that I simply wouldn't have made it through without you. My little sister Meg Leitold, you have been very supportive and thoughtful throughout this project, and I have valued it deeply. To all the Leitolds and Kings for welcoming me into your family, for your friendship and your generosity, thank you.

I also want to extend my gratitude to everyone who took the time to review all or part of the drafts of this manuscript, including Aleisha Cuff, Richard Laviolette (and thank you for your music!), Griffin Epstein, Mel Gayle, Stefanie Gude, Meg Leitold, Lisa Leinveer, Laura MacDonald, Andrew Mindszenthy, Lenny Olin, Sarah Vance, Lesley Wood and the three anonymous reviewers. Wayne Antony, thank you for your experienced and thoughtful guidance through this project while respecting my politics and my voice. I have had to frame my analysis in order to do educational workshops, which helped me frame this book. I am grateful to everyone who has planned and presented workshops with me over the years including (but I am probably missing people): Kandice Ferguson, Leah Dolmage, Meg Leitold, Ayshia Musleh, Caligula Ceasar and Amanda Dorter. Lastly, to Davie Parsons, thanks for your friendship and support.

Thanks also to the people at Fernwood who helped make this project corporeal. Thanks, especially, to the already-mentioned Wayne Antony, John van der Woude for the cover design and to Beverley Rach and Debbie Mathers for their production and pre-production expertise, respectively. Thanks also to Curran Faris for the thorough and detailed copyediting.

Chapter 1

Building Models and Constructing Disability

The fanciest party I ever threw was in celebration of the government officially recognizing me as disabled. Normally, such an occasion would have been met with extreme poverty, but not this day. This particular day was filled with pot pies, stuffed mushrooms, luxurious cheeses, wine and raspberry mousse in tiny chocolate cups. My declaration of disability came with a $12,000 cheque.

Like many things that come from the government, however, there were strings attached. I had to spend all but $5,000 in six months without acquiring any non-exempt assets (like a prepaid funeral or work tools), otherwise my disability cheque would be suspended. So, I went on a road trip with some friends to Dollywood in Pigeon Forge, Tennessee, bought a lot of things I needed but had gone without over the years, gave some money away, paid some bills and threw this party.

The party was a thank-you to the people in my community who had been generous with me over the years. These folks had let me come along in their (often rented) cars without asking me to pay for gas and eat their food without paying them back, or they were part of my care collective, helping me shop, clean, cook and do laundry when needed. I almost always met this generosity with frugality, because I was trying to get by on welfare (just over $500 a month) in Toronto, one of the most expensive cities in the country.

The cheque that made me a thousandaire was back-pay; it was money I was owed for the two-and-a-half years that it had taken to navigate the snail's-pace disability benefits system. The cheque didn't, of course, include the several years I had lived solely on welfare prior to submitting my disability application forms. I had repeatedly asked my doctor to complete my application, but each time she told me, "We'll have you better in six months." Six months later, I would ask again until, finally, she agreed.

Once my application was complete — including multiple letters from specialists, medical reports and my own personal statement — I sent it off and waited for nearly eight months, only to be denied. I knew in advance that this would happen. About half of those who apply for the Ontario Disability Support Program (ODSP), or "disability" as those of us who receive support often call it, are initially denied (West End Legal Services of Ottawa, 2009).

Notably, 60 percent of applications submitted are accepted on appeal (Social Benefits Tribunal, 2008-2009).

This increase in my income, nearly double the amount I received on welfare, means that things are much better for me; however, disability rates in Ontario are still poverty rates. A basic ODSP cheque amounts to roughly $100 more than the average rent of a one-bedroom apartment in Toronto.[1] A single person on ODSP has an income of only 71 percent of the poverty line.[2] I was on welfare for many years, just like the many disabled people who cannot find accessible work, who are waiting to receive ODSP or who don't qualify for ODSP. Currently, people on welfare have an income that is only 42 percent of the poverty line (Ministry of Community and Social Services, 2010).

Until the government classified me as disabled, for the sake of receiving disability benefits I operated in a legal realm where I was simultaneously disabled and not disabled. The government declaration that I was disabled under the law did not change anything about me, except my bank balance. For the purposes of human rights legislation and access to a seat at the front of the bus, I was disabled. These practices and policies, while important, provide few meaningful benefits to disabled people and have broad, inclusive definitions of disability. However, for the purposes of having enough money to live off of, I was not disabled. The definition of disabled to qualify for social assistance is incredibly narrow, so a very limited number of people receive any money.

It was this shifting nature of the definition of disability that got me interested in figuring out what exactly disability is. How is it that people can move back and forth, being disabled and non-disabled through a change in policy or medical definition, while nothing actually changes about their bodies or minds? How can someone be disabled and non-disabled at the same time?

The conclusion I came to is fairly simple: disability is a construct. Because disability, like other marginalities, is contextual, you cannot actually understand where disability is without understanding where disability has been. There is a great deal of diversity in how disability is viewed, depending on culture, place or period in time. The ways in which disability is perceived and defined fundamentally change depending on the context in which it is viewed in. The ways in which disability is viewed are always informed by class, gender, race and age, among other marginalities. While the definition of disability has shifted throughout time and varies with context, inherent to the definition is a sense of abnormality, a deviation from the norm. The norm, too, however, is culturally contingent.

Lennard J. Davis (1995: 24) writes that the "idea of a norm is less a condition of human nature than it is a feature of a certain kind of society." Davis also points out that the contemporary ideas of "normal" and "average" are relatively new. Until 1840, in fact, "normal" was only used in the mathematical sense, to mean perpendicular (Davis, 1995).

Models of Disability

This book argues that disability is a construct. Further, this book makes the case that disability is understood through models of thought and action; these models are pervasive at certain times or sites in culture. This book outlines six main models of inventing, understanding and managing the concept of disability within Western societies: the eugenic model, the medical model, the charity model, the rights model, the social model and, finally, the radical model. This list is by no means complete — there are many more models including, but not limited to, the individual model, the middle range adjustment model (Oliver, 1996), the social death model, the social barriers model, the administrative model (Finkelstein, 1993), the socio-medical model, the socio-political model (Turmusani, 2003), the personal tragedy model (Carlson, 2010), the social role valorization model (Wolfensberger, 2000), the cultural model (Devlieger et al., 2003), the affirmation model (Swain and French, 2000), the independent living model (Phillips, 2001), the moral (or karma) model (Bhanushali, 2007), the World Health Organization (WHO) model (Elliott and Dreer, 2007), the structural model, the minority model (Brown et al., 2009), the socio-spatial model (Gleeson, 1999), the holy innocent model, the subhuman organism model, the menace model and the developmental model (Stroman, 2003). Such a proliferation of models exist that Michael Oliver (1996: 31) said, "At one point it seemed that we would end up with more models than the Lucy Clayton Modelling Agency."

There are so many models for inventing and understanding disability because disability is not a fixed category. Rather, it is a fluid definition that depends not only on the context in which it is defined, but also who defines it. The models examined in this book are those I consider to be the most influential and/or important in Western society. The models of disability, however, do not have fixed borders; rather, they can be porous, bleeding into each other or reinforcing one another.

The foundations of the modern conceptualizations of disability were laid with the advent of eugenics. Eugenics is based in a belief that certain people are genetically superior to others and that people deemed inferior pollute the gene pool, diminishing the strength and desirability of the entire population. Eugenicists, fuelled by capitalist ideals and industrialist values, promote selective breeding in order to encourage population growth of desirable people and a reduction of undesirable people, until the latter are eliminated.

Eugenics created the first modern classification of disability. It continues to have a tremendous influence on views of disability today. Lennard J. Davis writes:

> Eugenics saw the possible improvement of the race as being accom-plished by diminishing problematic peoples and their problematic behaviors — these peoples were clearly delineated under the rubric of feeble-mindedness and degeneration as women, people of colour, homosexuals, the working class and so on. All these were considered to be categories of disability, although we do not think of them as connected in this way today. (2002: 14)

Originally, the concept of disability applied to any number of people who were considered to have genetically and socially undesirable traits. This broad definition of disability, upheld in the late 1800s and early 1900s, demonstrates how its categorization was used to further marginalize and control large groups of people and to enforce social norms.

The medical model of disability has been the primary paradigm for understanding disability since the decline of eugenics. The medical model views disability as an individual tragedy and as based within the body. Despite the medical model's seeming differences, it is not always distinct from eugenics; there was a great deal of overlap between the two during the height of eugenics. Today, the medical model often draws on eugenics and continues in its legacy.

There is sometimes a separation made between the medical model of disability and the rehabilitation model of disability. Both the medical model and the rehabilitation model are centred around individual bodies and minds and are invested in expert knowledge. The difference between the two, argues David Pfeiffer (2003), is that the medical model focuses on curing disability while the rehabilitation model focuses on diminishing, adapting or concealing disability. This model is, however, a derivative of the medical model (Pfeiffer, 2003). I do not think that the distinction between the medical model and rehabilitation is at all substantial enough to warrant a separate model and, as such, I discuss it within the framework of the medical model.

Complementary to the medical model is the charity model of disability. In its current form, the charity model reinforces the medical model, accepting medicalization as the primary way of defining disability. However, it provides a "softer side" to the mainstream approach to disability, framing disability as a tragedy and something that can be resisted. If enough people come together to walk/run/bowl/ride/sleep/fast/climb/gamble/skip/donate, disability can be "fought," ultimately eradicating disability and, therefore, disabled people.

Some have argued that the charity, medical and eugenic models are all components of an individual model of disability. For instance, Michael Oliver

(1996: 31) argues that "there is no such thing as the medical model of disability, there is instead, an individual model of disability of which medicalization is one significant component." For Oliver, who is one of the most influential disability studies scholars, there are only two models: the individual and the social. While Oliver would likely categorize the eugenic, medical and charity models together, there are important differences between them. Each model has different conceptualizations of disability, different actors and different effects. Oliver is right that these models all have an individual focus, and the boundaries between them may be blurry at the edges or they may overlap; however, the three models are distinct approaches to disability and warrant separate discussions.

In the 1970s, disabled activists reacted strongly and publicly to the eugenic, medical and charity models of disability. Disabled organizers in the United States and Canada responded to these brutal modes of understanding and managing disability by taking a rights-based approach. Activists in the United Kingdom created an entirely new model for understanding disability, the social model, which spread internationally. The rights model focused on accessing society, but, the social model focused on changing society. Both models, however, drew from other struggles and social movements.

The people who developed the social model were engaged in social action,` and their new discourse not only changed the conversation about disability, but also presented a new framework in which disabled people could be united and organized. As a result, the social model became highly influential in disability politics in North America and across the globe.

This new social model separated "disability" from "impairment," defining disability as the oppression imposed on disabled people as a result of our impairments (our diagnoses, or, in their terms, "defects," "limitations," etc.); the social model took the focus off of disabled people's individual "limitations" and focused on the inaccessibility of the built environment and society.

However, the social model has limitations and, in many circumstances, helps to perpetuate the oppression of disabled people. Thus I propose an alternative model for understanding disability, which I call the radical model. This model specifically takes up the social model's separation of impairment from disability, a false binary that was a useful explanatory tool at one time but has long since become a tool of continued oppression. We put social meaning onto people's bodies and minds. Impairment shifts depending on the context that it is experienced in. I do not argue that there is no biological function or reality at play with our minds and our bodies; we are physical beings. However, we put social meaning onto that biology, and we cannot separate the two. There is no such thing as a biological reality that creates impairment; impairment is socially constructed and imposed upon us, just as disability is.

While the social model has made very important and lasting contributions to the disabled community and the disability rights movement, it is time to rejoin disability and impairment and create a new disability paradigm. The radical disability model maintains that there is nothing wrong with us. We are only disabled because we are identified as such by existing power structures, as a way to keep those power structures intact.

While definitions and ways of understanding disability have changed, there is one commonality among disabled people, at least for the past century and a half in Western cultures. It is that "ideal" is white, straight, productive, profitable and patriarchal. Disabled people are labelled disabled because they — we — challenge the notion of the ideal. Radical disability politics is grounded in the belief that the systems that oppress us, not us, are fundamentally flawed.

These systems manipulate the definition of disability, depending on their needs, resulting in a constantly changing and shifting understanding of disability over time. Because disability is different in different cultures and contexts, in this book I speak only to the dominant Canadian and American constructions of disability (as the two are very similar). Perhaps when you picked up this book you had a specific idea about what disability was, but there is no universal definition of disability.

Disabled, Non-disabled and Disablism

All of the models of disability are used to define groups of people as disabled. Different groups of people are classified as disabled or not based on the model being used. But what do you call those of us who have been labelled as disabled? There are a number of different names that are, or have been, used for us, most of them oppressive. These days the acceptable terms are generally considered to be "people with disabilities" or "disabled people," and both are sometimes used interchangeably. Oftentimes, though, people use one or the other because they believe it to be correct.

The term "people with disabilities" is part of a broader lexicon called "people first language." The rationale for using this language, according to Kattie Snow, the mother of a person with a disability, is that "people with disabilities are people, *first*" (Snow, 2010: 1). Proponents of this language say "disabled" is an inappropriate word because of its other meanings: "broken/non-functioning" (Snow, 2010: 2). Disabled author Ruth Enns (1999: 90) argues the phrase is "an effort to put their human status ahead of their disabilities."

There are some major problems with the "people first" approach. This language often comes from people who are not disabled but claim to work in our interests (Oliver, 1990). The language also implies that disability is something separate and apart from personhood or humanity, unfortunate conditions attached to otherwise normal people. Other criticisms involve the ease of interchangeability of the word disability with medical diagnoses: people with autism, people with spinal muscular atrophy, people with schizophrenia, people with epilepsy, people with disabilities and so on. This is problematic because it lends itself so easily to medical discourse, something that many disabled people resist.

The phrase "disabled people" does not treat disability as passive or an afterthought. Disability exists as a consequence of an active process of marginalization — people *are* disabled. Disability is something that is imposed on us (Oliver, 1990, 1996, 2004). While the phrase has a negative connotation, I argue that disabled people have largely reclaimed it.

We are disabled. But what of those of us who are not categorized in this way? Within mainstream disability rights and public discourse in Canada and the United States, the term "able-bodied" has seeped into popular usage. This is a reflection of the dominance of physically disabled people within disability rights movements. Sometimes "temporarily able-bodied" (or TAB) is used to illustrate the fact that most people will be disabled at some point. Obviously, many people who are intellectually or psychiatrically disabled are erased from the disabled community if this term is used (Campbell and Oliver, 1996).

Contrary to popular understanding, however, all disabled people, including physically disabled people, can be, and are, disabled and able-bodied simultaneously. Indeed, "able-bodied" and "disabled" are not oppositional or necessarily even different. While I have a physical disability, I am alive because of my able body. I will not be able-bodied one day — that will be the day that I die. My body keeps me alive, it sustains me, it allows me to experience and perceive. I am able-bodied.

The opposite of disabled is simply non-disabled. However, this too is problematic because it presents disability as a clear category that everyone either falls into or outside of. The reality is that disability is in constant flux and people move in and out of the category depending on context. Margrit Shildrick (2009) points out that using the categories of disabled and non-disabled works to uphold the problematic and false binary and the systems that permit their creation. But, while the business of naming can be problematic, even contradictory, and language can limit the way we conceptualize things, it is an important starting point to building unity and creating space to work together.

The oppression that disabled people experience is disablism. Disablism is defined by Miller, Parker and Gillinson (2004: 9) as "discriminatory, oppressive or abusive behaviour arising from the belief that disabled people are inferior to others." Nevertheless, "ableism" is a word that is often used to describe our oppression. Sometimes people go back and forth between the two terms, but frequently word use is determined by geography. North Americans commonly use the term "ableism," while "disablism" is preferred by the British (Goodley, 2011; Ashby, 2010). However, I believe that ableism is a misnomer. Ableism implies that one is being oppressed because of (or a perceived lack of) ability when, in reality, one experiences oppression because of disability.

Privilege, Lip-Service and Social Change

While much of this book discusses various models of disability, a knowledge of theory is not particularly useful without action. I provide context and insight into disability and how and why it is constructed. But fundamentally, I hope that this book will incite people to take an active role in working for change that is inclusive of disability politics and disabled people.

It is imperative to note that I do not speak for disabled people. My experience, like that of all disabled people, is unique. I am white, while most disabled people are not. It is also impossible, at times, to separate where my disability begins and my transsexuality, poverty and queerness end, even though all of these things have, at times, also been considered disabilities. I also live with full immigration status in Canada. Canada is one of the richest countries in the world and much of the wealth held in this country originates from the stolen land, resources and cultures of First Nations people, who have rates of disability almost twice as high as the rest of the population in Canada (Human Resources and Skills Development Canada, 2007). Much of Canada's remaining wealth is derived from the theft of resorces from other Indigenous people around the world. I have a tremendous amount of privilege as a disabled person because I live in Canada, and my perspective informs my understanding of disability.

Another point of my privilege is that I can also pass as non-disabled a fair amount of the time if I so choose. When my life is such that I wouldn't pass as non-disabled, I am frequently unable to leave my house. Therefore, under certain circumstances, I can choose when, and to whom, to "come out" to as disabled.

My experience of disability is also informed by the fact that I am a political organizer and believe strongly that our systems of governance and economics are fundamentally flawed and cannot be reformed — rather, they should be overthrown. As an activist, being disabled has been a lonely and hard place.

When I began researching, writing about and working on disability politics, I understood that disability was, at best, tacked onto "the list" — the series of oppressions that "we" are against or people "we" are in solidarity with. I couldn't find books about disability in political bookstores, and no one I knew ever went to disabled people's protests or even knew they were happening. No one was talking about disability, and everyone in activist circles around me identified as or was assumed to be non-disabled.

One of the first times I really felt the impacts of the lip-service of "the list" was about ten years ago at a social justice conference for students. This was my second time doing an anti-disablism workshop, and it was the first time this type of workshop had ever been done at the annual conference. I went into the room early to set up an activity I had made. I taped up words like "gimp," "spaz," "blind," "lame," "schizo," "retard/ed," "dumb," "challenged" and "crazy," written on about twenty large pieces of paper all around the room. The activity involved having people draw several cards, on some of which were written the words people meant to say when they used these slurs, while the other cards had the definitions or origins of the words. The participants were to match the cards with the words on the walls, and then we would talk about language. The only person who came to the workshop was the woman who was supposed to introduce me. All of the ten-to-fifteen other organizers and the sixty or seventy participants of the conference chose to attend one of the other two workshops. Once she left the room, I sat down, surrounded by all the words that bombard and devalue disabled people. As the cards fluttered in the breeze from the central air, I began to cry.

After a while I got used to being asked to do workshops and having no one show up. Sometime after that, I started refusing to do them unless I was guaranteed that a certain number of people would be there, or that the workshop wouldn't be "competing" against other oppressed groups for an audience. I got tired of constantly being reminded that progressives didn't think disability or disabled people were important.

Over the past decade, however, I have seen an increase in people's level of engagement around disability issues. This excites me. Not only does there seem to be an increased awareness about disability issues, at least in some communities that I organize with, but there also seems to be a hunger developing amongst some disabled and non-disabled people for information and representation.

These days when I do workshops, people come. I often start them off by asking a series of questions. The first question is, "Do you identify as disabled?" In a room with fifty people in it, four or five will put up their hands. On reading the second question, "Are you identified or do you identify as disabled?" a few more hands will reluctantly rise. Before reading the lengthy third question, I ask people to not raise their hands until I am finished. Then, I ask:

> Do you have a psychiatric diagnosis, do you take psych meds, have you ever been under a "Community Treatment Order" or incarcerated in a psych facility? Have you been diagnosed with autism spectrum disorder, are you neuroatypical or neurodiverse? Do you have a terminal illness, a chronic illness, chronic fatigue or chronic pain? Are

you a foot fetishist? Do you have a genetic or congenital disease? Are you a drug addict or alcoholic? Do you use a wheelchair or mobility aid? Do you use braces, a cane or crutches, have difficulty walking or do not walk? Are you a transsexual? Do you have asthma? Are you an amputee? Are you intersexed and currently have non-gender conforming genitals and/or appearance? Do you have a learning, intellectual or cognitive disability? Are you fat? Are you Deaf or hard of hearing? Are you blind or do you have low vision? Are you HIV positive or do you have AIDS? Are you a heterosexual male who cross-dresses and is severely distressed by it, or are you gay and severely distressed by it?

When I tell people to raise their hands, usually well over half of the room, and, on occasion, the whole room, puts their hands up, some proudly and others very reluctantly.

Finally, I ask, "Did you answer 'yes' to any of the questions that have been asked, or could you have but you didn't because of stigma, fear, shame, apathy or any other reason?" At this point the number of hands in the air has multiplied dramatically from the first question, and I tell everyone that this is who I am talking about when I talk about disabled people. Of course, this list is incomplete and there are problems with this exercise, but I think it is a useful demonstration.[3]

While I do think there has been an improvement over the years in the number of people who are concerned with disability issues, it is important for non-disabled activists to understand that it is hard for many disabled activists to extend trust after generations of exclusion and erasure.

One of the causes of this mistrust is that, for the most part, our histories have been deleted from the history of the Left. Disabled people like Rosa Luxemburg and Antonio Gramsci have had their disabilities erased or diminished, or, as Helen Keller exemplifies, their radical politics have been erased. Direct actions by the disability rights movement have not been celebrated, studied or replicated in the ways that actions by other movements have been. And, perhaps most significantly, the complicity of the Left in disabled peoples' marginalization has been largely omitted from historical accounts of social justice movements. Adding us to "the list" is relatively meaningless as long as there is no acknowledgment of this rewritten history and the resulting, and legitimate, skepticism of radical movements by disabled people.

Perhaps one of the primary reasons that disabled people have been actively excluded from the Left is because there is an unspoken belief, held by other Leftists, that we are broken or flawed. Douglas Baynton writes:

Rarely have oppressed groups denied that disability is an adequate justification for social and political inequality. Thus, while disabled people can be considered one of the minority groups historically assigned inferior status and subjected to discrimination, disability has functioned for all such groups as a sign of and justification for inferiority. (2001: 34)

Such conclusions are often made without talking to disabled people. There is an assumption that disablism is not a form of oppression to the same degree as other forms of oppressions because it is somehow justified, and thus, no effort is made to make meetings socially, linguistically or physically accessible. No resources are allocated to anti-disablism education, and no space is created to hear about disability or to listen to disabled people. Therefore, nothing is learned about our lives, and our experiences as oppressed people continue to be devalued.

Social justice can never be achieved without working with disabled people and on disability issues. The construction of disability is an essential tool for how people with power work to maintain that power. Without targeting disability specifically and simultaneously recognizing and responding to its intersectionality with other oppressions, the systems and values that create disability will remain intact, replicating disablism.

Similarly, disabled people, who often organize apart from the rest of the Left, cannot expect to be victorious in fighting for justice without resisting other forms of oppression. Most disabled people have at least two points of marginality. Most of us are women, racialized, poor, queer or any such combination. Internationally, the vast majority of disabled people are racialized (New Internationalist, 2005; Parens et al., 2009).[4] Further, in Canada most disabled people are women (Federal, Provincial and Territorial Advisory Committee on Population Health, 1999; Raphael, 2007). Disabled people are not a homogenous group; we are diverse and impacted by different oppressions. We cannot successfully (or conscionably) fight for the insertion of disability into mainstream society at the expense of others, particularly because most disabled people would be left behind in such a struggle.

While I have written extensively about theory, I have done it in this context of intersecting oppressions and struggles and with an understanding of the urgency of the need for change. This book is similarly situated. While we desperately need more education around disability issues, we need action just as much or more. We need people to organize their communities and to build movements. So, read on and resist!

Notes

1. ODSP rates for a single person as of December 2010: $1,053 (Income Support Advocacy Centre, 2010). Average one bedroom apartment rent: $949 (Settlement. org, 2010).
2. The poverty line in this instance is the Statistics Canada after-tax low-income cut-off.
3. Of course, there are problems with any exercise that involves participants raising their hands. While I encourage people to indicate in a number of different ways, (e.g., have myself, or a friend or neighbour raise a hand for them if they cannot or do not feel comfortable doing it themselves) some people may not be able or be comfortable to participate in such an exercise.
4. While these reports only talk about the high prevalence of disability in the "majority world," both logically and mathematically, one can only conclude that the majority of disabled people in the world are racialized.

Chapter 2

Constructing Difference, Controlling Deviance

The Eugenic Model

Eugenics is the belief that human evolution can be crafted by the encouraged breeding of people who are considered the most desirable — the "fit" — and the discouraged breeding of those who are considered the least desirable — the "unfit." Eugenics is inspired by evolutionary theory and operates under the assumption that humans can shape our own evolution in positive ways by engaging in selective breeding. The word itself is a creation of Sir Francis Galton, the father of eugenics, and is based on the Greek word *eugenes,* meaning well born or good stock. While Galton's theories were first published in 1865, he did not coin the word eugenics until 1883 in *Inquiries into Human Faculty and Its Development.* The word Galton used prior to eugenics was "viriculture" (Galton, 1907).

There are different ways of going about achieving eugenic goals and they are generally defined as either "negative" or "positive" eugenics. Negative eugenics focuses on the reduction of reproduction amongst those who are considered undesirable; positive eugenics focuses on increasing reproduction of those who are considered desirable. Further, eugenicists also differentiate between forms of eugenic programs. These programs can happen through insidious forms of control or coercion of reproduction, called passive eugenics, or through active eugenics — the implementation of programs that force eugenics onto people (such as through sterilizations, prohibitions in marriages, segregation and murder).

In 1865, Galton formulated the theory of eugenics, and with it the first cohesive ideas about a class of disabled people, or the unfit, were born in modern Western society. Galton saw eugenics both as "the science of improving inherited stock, not only by judicious matings, but by all the influences which give more suitable strains a better chance" and as a way "to give the more suitable races... a better chance of prevailing speedily over the less suitable" (in Galton and Galton, 1998: 99). Galton strongly believed that unfit people were reproducing at an alarming rate. He wanted to see "the undesirables be got rid of and the desirables multiplied" (in Black, 2003: 16). Of course, Galton's views of fitness, or disability, were based on the social, cultural and economic views at the time.

The eugenic model conceptualized disability as being in the individual body and as inheritable. Simply, disabled people were unfit: unfit to live in society, unfit to exist. Eugenicists believed eugenics offered a "solution" to disability, a way to eradicate disability from society. This model envisioned disability as a threat to society and to those considered fit. Primarily, eugenics honed in on all of those individuals who were struggling in society (almost always as a result of existing social injustices), labelled them as disabled and targeted them for eradication. The eugenic model constructed disability with such rabid contempt that its proponents would, and did, do anything to get rid of the problem disabled people posed, including murder.

The early part of the twentieth century saw an explosion in support for eugenics. A boon to the cause occurred when Galton's cousin, Charles Darwin, publicly declared his support for eugenics (Wikler, 1999). Eugenic organizations were established, including the American Breeders' Association's Eugenics Committee (1906) (Kimmelman, 1983), the United Farm Women of Alberta (1916) (Nind, 2000), the English Eugenics Education Society (1907) (Wikler, 1999) and the Racial Hygiene Society (Germany, 1905) (Wikler, 1999). A number of prominent people were involved in these organizations early on, including Alexander Graham Bell, Stanford professor Vernon Kellog, U.S. Assistant Secretary of Agriculture Willet M. Hayes, Dutch geneticist Hugo de Vries (Kimmelman, 1983), activist and soon-to-be Alberta MLA Irene Parlby, German biologist Alfred Ploetz (Black, 2003) and, of course, Francis Galton (Kevles, 1985). Eugenic movements also sprang up around the same time in Brazil, Norway and Russia, among many other places (Wikler, 1999).

The eugenic movement had its peak in the 1930s and 1940s and declined after the defeat of the Nazis, who had implemented horrific mass eugenic policies. However, eugenics made up the foundation of the modern Western understanding of disability, and its influences can be found in other mainstream models of disability. Some of the eugenic attitudes about disabled people and their reproduction remain present today.

Who Is "Fit" and Who Isn't

The eugenic worldview was a binary one in which there were two classes of people: those considered "fit" and those considered "unfit." The unfit class created the foundation for what is considered disability today. Who is considered disabled today, along with women, racialized people, homosexuals, queers, poor and working class people, were all considered disabled under eugenics(Davis,

2002). All of these attributes were considered to be negative and perceived to be inheritable, thus they were all presumed to be physical conditions. The elimination of these conditions — the elimination of disability, eugenicists believed — would lead to a more productive and far less troubled society.

Feeble-mindedness had a number of different definitions. One of these definitions was being unable to finish third grade (Pfeiffer, 1993). This definition failed to problematize the education system, the discrimination within it or any of the social factors that would prevent children from being able to attend or remain in school. Eugenicist Amos Butler (1921: 390) wrote, "Feeble-mindedness is one of the most potential [sic] destructive factors in our civilization. It produces more pauperism, more crime, more degeneracy, than any other one force." This ideology put the blame of social problems directly on those people who experienced the brunt of those problems. Therefore, eugenic ideas were highly popular amongst the upper (and growing middle) classes as eugenics explained away social problems by blaming the people who were the most negatively impacted by existing oppressions. The solution? Eliminate the people who cause the problems. With eugenics, there was no need for systemic change, only a change in who was a part of society.

Many of the eugenic solutions were adopted from Reverend Thomas Malthus. Malthus, a British author who wrote extensively about population, economics and politics in the late eighteenth and early nineteenth centuries, called for a widespread reduction in the global population. Malthus argued for the removal of poor laws and of the meagre poor-assistance systems of the time. He believed giving assistance to the poor would encourage them to have more children; thus, the population would increase, ultimately resulting in famine and war. Malthus (1888: 430) said, "We are bound in justice and honour formally to disclaim the *right* of the poor to support." Malthus held that the poor should be removed from society by encouraging death and disease:

> We should sedulously encourage the other forms of destruction, which we compel nature to use. Instead of recommending cleanliness to the poor, we should encourage contrary habits. In our towns we should make the streets narrower, crowd more people into the houses, and court the return of the plague. In the country, we should build our villages near stagnant pools, and particularly encourage settlements in all marshy and unwholesome situations. But above all, we should reprobate specific remedies for ravaging diseases; and those benevolent, but much mistaken men, who have thought they were doing a service to mankind by projecting schemes for the total extrapolation of particular disorders. (1888: 412)

He went on to argue that increased mortality would reduce the population to a sustainable level that would not result in mass hunger.[1] From a eugenic perspective, it was not only acceptable to permit people to live in abject poverty, it was preferred. This would allow evolution to take its course and cull those considered unfit.

It was no coincidence that the eugenic movement developed shortly after the industrial revolution, as it provided the perfect explanation for massive disparities in wealth as well as the increasing poverty and suffering among the working class. Eugenics provided those with power a justification for that power as well as a rationalization for the injustices and inequalities that industrial capitalism and colonialism brought forth in new and increasingly violent ways.

The unfit were largely classified as such because they were considered unproductive or underproductive within the capitalist economy. Leonard Darwin (1926: 366) argued that eugenic targets included "the immoral, the inefficient, the stupid, the unemployable, the weakly, etc." Many years later, eugenicist Frederick Osborn (1968: 105) would assert, "Achievement in building a home as well as success in other aspects of life constitutes a eugenic criterion." These statements illustrate the true motives of eugenic thought: to legitimize the oppression of groups of people by identifying them as defective, unfit and disabled, and to use that legitimacy to perpetuate oppression.

Eugenics formed a seemingly scientific way to establish an "other" and to legitimize "othering" — the process of establishing a group identity by stigmatizing and devaluing certain people. The individual and multiple identities of people who were labelled as "other" were replaced by one (negative) group identity or trait. Eugenics created the other as the unfit and targeted them for elimination.

Within eugenics, economic or political realities such as poverty are not caused by injustice but by genetically inherited traits. Social conditions and economic inequalities were considered individual heritable failings. Charles Davenport, one of the most prominent American eugenicists, argued that poor people were genetically unable to participate in competitive capitalist economies and support themselves. Davenport wrote:

> [There are many people] who lack one or more traits that are necessary for them to take their part in forwarding the world's work under the conditions of competition afforded by the society in which they live. If they fail in their part they become private or public charges or a social menace. (1912a: 53)

This would make them unfit. Leonard Darwin, another well-known eugenics supporter and the son of Charles Darwin, also argued that social problems, such as poverty, were directly related to one's genetic or physical make-up:

Does not the housing difficulty in most cases merely indicate the impossibility of an economic rent being paid, an impossibility often due to an actual incapacity on the part of the tenant to do work equivalent in value to what is needed to supply a decent dwelling? (1926: 387)

From a eugenic perspective, one's ability to support oneself within the capitalist system was hereditary, and poverty and "pauperism" (begging or taking charity out of poverty) were biologically predetermined.

Racialized people received special notice from eugenicists. In the late nineteenth and early twentieth centuries, this category consisted of a number of ethnicities that are now considered white, including Irish people, Jewish people and Eastern European immigrants. This category of racialized people also consisted of groups who continue to be considered people of colour, Black people being the most vehemently targeted. These groups were entirely, or almost entirely, poor; therefore, they were seen as undesirable and unworthy. (Alternatively, they were seen as undesirable and unworthy so they were entirely, or almost entirely, poor). Galton established a ranking system for determining a person's fitness in which Black people were automatically ranked two grades lower than what he considered to be the least-fit white person (Province, 1973). Edward East, in the 1919 text *Inbreeding and Outbreeding*, wrote that Black people were inferior to white people:

In reality the negro is inferior to the white. This is not hypothesis or supposition; it is a crude statement of actual fact. The negro has given the world no original contribution of high merit. By his own initiative in his original habitat, he has never risen.... In competition with the white race, he has failed to approach its standard (253).

Racialized groups were often considered lazy as well. A 1931 genetics text reported that "in general, a Negro is not inclined to work hard" (in Beckwith, 1993: 327).

At the First International Eugenics Congress (held in London, in 1912) Davenport argued for the separation of racialized groups from white society because they "do not go well with our social organization"(1912b: 154). Davenport continued:

For the Ethiopian has not undergone that selection that in Europe weeded out the traits that failed to recognize property rights, or that failed to give industry, ambition and sex control.[2] (1912b: 154)

Racist stereotypes and cultural differences, including understandings of property ownership, were all taken by eugenicists to be genetic faults or disabilities inherent to specific races or ethnic groups.

For eugenicists, racism and poverty were not social or economic problems; rather, they were natural and appropriate outcomes brought about by a host of inheritable defects. Capitalist colonial expansion, for which the appropriation of labour and land was essential, was justified by the believed natural inferiority of different groups. After all, Africans did not have the gene to respect property rights; therefore it wasn't really *their* land that was being stolen. This eugenic logic would have likely also extended to legitimize other colonial projects throughout the rest of the world.

The other groups that Davis (2002: 14) identifies as falling into "the rubric of feeble-mindedness and degeneration" were similarly categorized to legitimize social injustices. Homosexuals (and other gender transgressors[3]) were seen as deviant; however, there were competing eugenic arguments as to why. Some, like prominent eugenicist Havelock Ellis, thought they were genetically inferior and if they reproduced they would breed degenerate children (Ordover, 2003). Others, like psychiatrist George Henry, believed that homosexuals who were from a sound genetic stock would not reproduce because of their homosexuality, posing a eugenic threat (Terry, 1995).

Women were also eugenic targets; however, they were targeted differently depending on their social position. Rich and poor women were seen very differently in the late nineteenth and early twentieth centuries and were not categorized on any similar terms. Poor women were seen as a "different species" than rich women, according to Barbara Ehrenreich and Deirdre English in *Complaints and Disorders* (1976: 12). Poor women engaged in paid work and were frequently seen as carriers of disease. Because they were markedly different than rich women, it seems that much of the emphasis was put on their poverty. Under eugenic theory, however, they were paid special attention to because of the reproductive threat they posed: after all, they were the ones who brought even more poor children into the world.

Rich women (who were almost entirely, if not entirely, white) were pathologized in order to ensure the continuation and justification of sexism and patriarchy. Comments such as, "The man who does not know sick women does not know women," made by Dr. S Weir Mitchell, reflected the sentiment of the time (in Ehrenreich and English, 1976: 25). This pathologization of women, according to Ehrenreich and English (23), "seemed to take the malice out of sexual oppression: when you prevented a woman from doing anything active or interesting, you were only doing this for her own good."

Intellectually disabled people were also seen as unproductive, particularly in an increasingly industrial economy where work became more segmented and/or cognitively based (Harder and Scott, 2005). While there was an integrated place for both physically and intellectually disabled people before the eugenic period, these people began to be viewed as "useless and unproductive" with the rise of industrial capitalism (Tait, 1985–86: 451). This was the case, largely, because of disablist notions of productivity and the absence of accommodations for disabled workers, such as adjusting factory speeds, having a variety of training approaches, having a variety of time prompts and providing retraining as needed.

The groups that were targeted as eugenically unfit were targeted in ways that legitimized the status quo, propped up capitalism and justified the continued oppression of these groups out of biological necessity. All of these groups made up the original definition of disabled and were vilified and targeted as a result. "Feeble-minded" was not simply a politically incorrect turn of phrase — it was a label imposed on people to at once target certain groups and justify the systems that created them as separate in the first place.

Reducing the Unfit: Immigration

Eugenicists were determined to use any tool they could to reduce the populations of those they considered unfit. They had a number of successes in influencing governmental policies in Canada and the United States, particularly in keeping people they considered undesirable out of the country. In Canada, the 1886 *Immigration Act* prohibited "the landing in Canada of any immigrant or other passenger who is suffering from any loathsome, dangerous or infectious disease or malady" (in Chee, 1905: headnote). An earlier version of the law called for the screening of "imbeciles, idiots and morons" (in Gillis, 2001: A13).

The United States established similar policies of discrimination against disabled immigrants. In 1882, the federal government implemented a policy permitting the denial of entry to individuals who would potentially become a "public ward" (in Jaeger and Bowman, 2005: 51). Medical exams for immigration purposes were initiated nine years later (Fairchild and Tynan, 1994) because a key aim of immigration policy was to exclude disabled people (Longmore, 2003). As of 1917, people could be barred for things like varicose veins, asthma, hernias, poor eyesight, flat feet and a gamut of other conditions; further, beginning in 1949, an individual could have their immigrant status in the United States revoked if a medical condition that was missed at the border was subsequently discovered (Jaeger and Bowman, 2005).

These policies, coupled with clearly racist policies that established quotas for immigrants from certain countries, meant that most physically or intellectually disabled, racialized, and/or poor people would not be granted entry into either Canada or the United States.

Sterilization

While keeping disabled people out was effective, it did not address the many unfit people who were already within the country's borders. To do this, eugenicists focused their attention on limiting the reproduction of the unfit, specifically, through sterilization. Eugenics was not simply a way of understanding disability — it was a call to action, compelling its followers to urgently act to save the sanctity of the race. The United States enacted its first sterilization legislation in Indiana in 1907 (Kevles, 1985). In all, about 70,000 people were legally and forcibly sterilized between 1907 and 1970 (Black, 2003). Of the thirty-three states with eugenic sterilization legislation, twenty-six had it in place by 1932 (Davis, 1990).

The United States Supreme Court first addressed the issue of forced sterilization in the 1927 *Buck v. Bell* case. In this case, the court allowed the sterilization of a woman who had been labelled as feeble-minded. This was done despite arguments that the order would violate the woman's constitutional rights. Justice Holmes saw his decision as a benefit to society:

> It is better for all the world, if instead of waiting to execute degenerate offspring for crime, or to let them starve for their imbecility, society can prevent those who are manifestly unfit from continuing their kind. The principle that sustains compulsory vaccination is broad enough to cover cutting the Fallopian tubes…. Three generations of imbeciles are enough. (1927: 207)

Thus the U.S. Supreme Court legally legitimized eugenics by finding that that the interests of the state, and those of the capitalist driven economy, superseded individual rights. The eugenic model was upheld by the state and the eradication of disabled people became one of its goals.

In Canada, the Ontario government tried to impose forced sterilization legislation on people in 1912, but it did not pass (Kevels, 2000). Alberta and British Columbia were more successful, each passing a *Sexual Sterilization Act,* in 1928 and 1933, respectively. Both provinces established eugenics boards to approve sterilizations of disabled or unfit people.[4] In Alberta, the *Sexual Sterilization Act* was enacted (according to George Hoadley, the bill's sponsor) to address the "need for the state to be protected from the menace which the propagation by the mentally diseased brings about" (Robertson, 1996: n.p.). The *Act* called for sterilization in instances where there was a risk of "the transmission of any mental disability or deficiency to his progeny, or the risk of mental injury either to such person or his progeny" (*Muir v. Alberta*, 1996). The legislation had a specific apparatus to determine who should be sterilized on the grounds of their perceived disability.

Alberta's Eugenics Board viewed itself as a social enforcer and used its power to eliminate undesirable members of society (even beyond what had been established in the legislation). The sterilization of individuals who did not meet the criteria set out in the law and the use of sterilization as punishment for difficult or deviant prison inmates are but a few of the abuses carried out through the *Sexual Sterilization Act*. Many disabled women had their uterus and/or ovaries removed in order to eliminate menstruation. These women, according to the Board, proved "difficult to handle and to keep clean during menstrual periods," or masturbated or showed "lesbian tendencies" (*Muir v. Alberta*, 1996: para 53). By approving the use of sterilization, the overzealous Eugenics Board was in reality deciding who was disabled and who should be permitted to reproduce. After 1930, the Board approved sterilizations in ten minutes or less (*Muir v. Alberta*, 1996). In keeping with the logic of eugenics, sterilizations were often fuelled by sexist, racist and classist goals (Robertson, 1996). Towards the end of the Albertan eugenic program, one-quarter of all sterilizations were performed on First Nations and Métis people even though they made up less thant 3 percent of the population (Black, 2003).

Because it was permanent, sterilization was the first choice for most eugenicists dealing with the genetic "threat" posed by the unfit. However, the growing birth control movement attracted eugenicists as well. There was an affinity between early feminists — most of whom were straight, white, middle- and upper-class — and eugenicists around the issues of birth control. Feminists saw eugenics as an opportunity to build support for their campaign for access to birth control information and instruments (or they saw birth control as an opportunity to promote eugenics). While birth control was not permanent, it had the potential to dramatically reduce the reproduction of eugenically targeted populations. Birth control could also become something that many women who were considered unfit would embrace, unlike sterilization.

Feminist Complicity

With women as eugenic targets, first-wave feminists' adoption of the eugenic discourse presented not only the potential to win greater capacity to control their own reproduction, but also an opportunity to remove themselves out from under the eugenic umbrella. Early feminist campaigns endeavoured to overcome the fact that they had been labelled as disabled on account of their female "affliction" and to gain access to the same privileges as the rest of society. These campaigns worked to reinforce the oppression of all those groups that they left behind, including poor people, racialized people, homosexuals, queer and trans people and those who are still thought of as disabled today.

In fact, eugenics became front and centre in the discourse of the feminist campaign for birth control. One prominent feminist, Charlotte Perkins Gilman, said, "An active sense of social motherhood is desperately needed among women of today, if we are to put a stop to war, to cease producing defectives and to begin the conscious improvement of our stock" (in May 1995: 70). Victoria Woodhull (1893: 278) condemned the building of institutions and hospitals because "medical experts do all they can to keep alive the unfit brought together in these institutions, and destined, should they survive, to perpetuate a deteriorated race." Two of Canada's most famous suffragists, Nellie McClung and EmilyMurphy, adamantly supported eugenics. These two women were integral in the campaign for Alberta's *Sexual Sterilization Act* (Devereaux, 2005; Grekul, 2008).

Margaret Sanger, likely the most famous of the early feminists, passionately campaigned for both birth control and eugenics. Initially, her focus was most strongly placed on women's right to limit their family size; however, she later began openly advocating for the implementation of sweeping eugenic policies. Sanger called for "a stern and rigid policy" in which the government would "give certain dysgenic groups in our population their choice of segregation or sterilization" (in Carlson, 2010: 82). Sanger (1925: 5) also argued that "the Government of the United States deliberately encourages and even makes necessary by its laws the breeding — with a breakneck rapidity — of idiots, defectives, diseased, feeble-minded and criminal classes."

Eugenic ideas were not limited to a few first-wave feminists; rather, eugenics was a core component of first-wave feminism. The National Council of Women of Canada (1893) (Roberts, 1979), National League of Women Voters (1920) (Lemons, 1990), American Birth Control League (1921) (Ordover, 2003), Birth Control Clinical Research Bureau (1923) (Engs, 2000), Canadian Birth Control League (1924) (Prentice, 1988), Planned Parenthood (1942) (Kline, 2001)[5] and Birthright Inc. (1943) (Robitsche, 1973) were early feminist groups; they were all founded by women, promoted some level of women's rights, had platforms founded on eugenic principles and worked diligently to have eugenic politics implemented.

By adopting eugenics, feminists effectively expanded their base of support and garnered support for the right to vote (as well as other rights) where they may not have had that support previously. For example, Robert Reid Rentoul, in the 1906 book *Race Culture or Race Suicide*, supported first-wave feminism because it was serving a eugenic purpose. Rentoul (1906: 47) said, "A great many of our social problems can only be dealt with if women will take up their proper position in public affairs, and give their time and attention to questions which men generally have little wish to tackle." A number of prominent men supported birth control as a feminist demand because these women successfully argued that birth control was an important eugenic tool that would assist in limiting the birth rate of those labelled as disabled.

Not only did the birth control campaign earn the burgeoning white, middle- and upper-class feminist movement an early win,[6] it also took these women out of what Davis (2002: 14) called "the rubric of feeble-mindedness" and into a new category of person. This person was the modern woman, a voter, for whom this era of feminism was built — the rich, white, straight woman, not yet equal, but on her way. As a part of this move towards the idea of the modern woman, these women worked to reinforce the notion that there was nothing wrong with (or disabled) about themselves by arguing that there was something seriously and dangerously wrong with the real disabled people: the poor, the racialized, the queer, the psychiatrized, the intellectually disabled and the physically disabled. As a result of the feminist movement, the eugenic model was recast. Privileged women were removed from the cage of disability in exchange for guarding the door.

By 1933, first-wave feminism was well established as a vehicle for eugenics. Birth control was increasingly widespread and eugenic sterilizations were taking place in large parts of North America and Europe. Additionally, forty-two American states had laws prohibiting interracial marriage; at least twenty-five of the state laws could result in a prison or hard labour sentence. In Pennsylvania, any free Blacks could be ordered back into servitude if they were convicted of violating the interracial marriage law (Newbeck, 2004).

From a eugenic perspective, forced sterilization, birth control and anti-marriage laws for interracial couples appear to have been quite successful in reducing populations that were considered disabled. In the period from 1800 to 1820, there were ninety-three Black people for every one hundred white people in the United States. Between 1900 and 1920, there were forty-four Black people for every one hundred white people (Wilcox, 1922). Additionally, in 1910, Black women's reproduction rates dropped to two-thirds of what they had been in 1880 (Roberts, 1997). Some of the reduction in the proportion of Black population was caused by sterilization and restrictive, racist immigration legislation. Poverty, low life expectancy rates and other factors also worked to reduce Black populations.

Nazi Eugenics

Canadian and American eugenic projects were well underway by the time Adolf Hitler was elected German Chancellor in 1933. Nazi Germany, under Hitler's leadership, adopted eugenic aims as state policy, initially copying many North American programs (Black, 2003). Yet, this was not the first time Germany initiated eugenic policy. During World War I, the country starved tens of thousands of psychiatrized people to death — they were simply too low on the priority list to receive rations (Lifton, 1986). Under Hitler, the systemic starvation of disabled people and other "useless eaters" became official state policy (Lifton,1986) after a prolonged propaganda campaign to stigmatize these people as "life unworthy of life" (in Rees, 2005: 177).

Hitler operated under the common eugenic belief that "those who are physically and mentally unhealthy and unfit must not perpetuate their own suffering in the bodies of their children … it is a crime and a disgrace to make this affliction all the worse by passing on disease and defects to innocent creatures out of mere egoism" (Hitler, 1939: 243). The Nazis passed the *Law for the Prevention of Offspring with Hereditary Diseases* on July 14, 1933 (Biesold, 1999). While the precise number of people sterilized under the law will never be known, it is estimated that 200,000 to 375,000 people were sterilized on the grounds of hereditary disease (Lifton, 1986; Biesold, 1999).[7] Those targeted for sterilization were people with a number of what were considered to be hereditary diseases: psychiatric diagnoses, feeble-mindedness, blindness, Deafness, Huntington's disease, epilepsy, deformation and alcoholism (Lifton, 1986). Beyond sterilization, disabled women in Nazi Germany were also subjected to forced abortions at any time during the pregnancy. The numbers of these torturous procedures are unknown; however, there are fifty-seven documented cases of Deaf women who were subjected to this horror (Biesold, 1999).

Sterilization and forced abortion, however, weren't enough. Just before World War II started, Hitler decreed the expansion of "the authority of individual physicians, with the view to enable them, after the most critical examination in the realm of human knowledge, to administer to incurably sick persons a mercy death" (in Arad, 1987: 9). This began the Nazi euthanasia programs. The word "euthanasia" is from the Greek meaning "good death" and is a clear misnomer in relation to the Nazi murders: doctors starved, gassed and drugged their patients to death.

Some doctors approached the executions with a morbid creativity. It was doctors who came up with the idea to make the gas chambers appear to be shower rooms so people would be willing to enter them (O'Neil, 2001). Throughout the Holocaust, hundreds of thousands of disabled people who had previously been targeted by the Nazis for sterilization were actually killed (O'Neil, 2001). While the numbers of people killed because of their medical diagnoses will never be known, an estimated 200,000 to 250,000 people were killed under the Nazi's T-4 program (Friedman, 2004), including 85,000 to 105,000 inmates of mental institutions, 5,000 of them children (Lifton, 1986).

Many disabled people who were targeted by the Nazis are largely excluded from these numbers as well. As Sandy O'Neil (2001: 69), author of the comprehensive *First They Killed the 'Crazies' and the 'Cripples'* writes, "Even taking low figures, demographically about 10 percent of any given population have some types of disabilities. This would mean 600,000 Jews with disabilities at a minimum."

To further complicate this position, in the context of Nazi society, being disabled and being Jewish could not be distinguished. At the time, to be Jewish was to be disabled. Hitler (1939: 243) wrote of Jews as having "the blood of an inferior stock." One's "Jewishness" was a part of the body, a blood disease that resulted in a number of physical and mental symptoms.

This argument is not an attempt to diminish the rabid anti-Semitism of Hitler and the Nazi Party; indeed, most Jews never would have been classified as eugenically unfit or disabled if not for anti-Semitism. Undeniably, six million Jews were killed because they were Jewish. In addition to being Jewish, however, they were also disabled under the eugenic model, which was grounds for killing someone. Within eugenic logic, it is impossible to parse apart disability from race, ethnicity, anti-sociality or sexual orientation — they are all categorized, albeit with different implications, as a form of unfit or deviant identity that lives in the body and in nature.

While the international community found the extermination of many groups abhorrent, this moral outrage was generally not extended to disabled people because of other countries' treatment of and attitudes toward disabled people. Germany would not pay out any compensation to those who were sterilized because the Nazis were considered to have legitimate genetic reasons (O'Neil, 2001). Eugenic sterilizations continued in Canada, the United States, Sweden, Denmark, Finland and Switzerland after World War II (Spallone, 1989).

North American Eugenics After World War II

Following World War II, there was public recoil against eugenics. The graphic and horrifying images that came out of Germany from the Holocaust largely made eugenics distasteful. However, sterilization programs remained in practice. This may indicate a shift in the eugenic model's conceptualization of disability from marginality as disability to (so-called) legitimate genetic defect as disability, which would later bleed into the medical model.

Alberta's *Sexual Sterilization Act* was only repealed in 1972 after 2,822 people had been legally sterilized (*Muir v. Alberta*, 1996). British Columbia's program was never implemented on the same scale as that of Alberta's. In B.C., there are 188 documented cases of people who were forcibly sterilized in the Essondale Provincial Mental Hospital before the law was repealed in 1973 (*E.(D.) v. R.*, 2003).[8] Between 1940 and 1979 about 35,000 people were sterilized under eugenic legislation in the United States (Black, 2003).[9]

These programs continued until the 1970s in many areas, but there were exceptions. In 1975 North Carolina enacted forced sterilization legislation, which was not repealed until 2003 (Silver, 2003–2004). At least seven other states: Arkansas, Delaware, Georgia, Idaho, Mississippi, Vermont and Virginia continued to have sterilization legislation after the turn of this century (Silver, 2003–2004). While forced sterilization legislation was largely discontinued in the United States, eugenic sterilizations remained a regular occurrence. Most of these sterilizations were done to Black women, and many were performed without their knowledge.

Forced sterilizations continued in large numbers in the 1970s. Programs financed by the federal government resulted in the sterilization of 100,000 to 150,000 women a year in the early 1970s, and almost half of these women were Black (Black, 2003). In 1972 alone, however, there were 200,000 sterilizations (Davis, 1990). Many of these sterilizations occurred on the threat of withdrawal of social assistance (Roberts, 1997).

America, over two decades after the Holocaust, was achieving steriliza- tion rates of the same magnitude that Nazi Germany had accomplished (Roberts, 1997). President Nixon reportedly believed that Black people, due to their genetic inferiority, would barely benefit from federal programming (Ehrlichman, 1982). However, the government was willing to spend a mas- sive amount on their forced sterilization. And, by the early 1970s, a quarter of First Nations women living on reservations in the United States had been sterilized (Ehrlichman, 1982). The American government helped finance an even more successful eugenic sterilization program in Puerto Rico, which by 1968 saw the sterilization of one-third of all women there (Roberts, 1997).[10] The targeting of the eugenically unfit continued, albeit more surreptitiously, after the fall of the Nazis.

Today in the United States, coerced sterilization remains commonplace. The lack, or inaccessibility, of state and federal funding for abortions means that many women cannot afford to get abortions even if they wanted one. Angela Davis (1990: 17) argues this policy has "effectively divested [poor women] of the right to legal abortions. Since surgical sterilizations... remained free on demand, more and more poor women have been forced to opt for permanent infertility." While these sterilizations may not be legally forced, many women feel that they have no other options because of governmental policies.

The organization Project Prevention operates openly in the United States. Project Prevention pays women who are drug users or alcoholics $300 to get permanently sterilized. Project Prevention founder Barbara Harris (2009) says that "what separates this organization from many others is that we work to prevent a problem rather than spending the money we receive to treat one."

An ad on Project Prevention's website shows a very young baby covered with a number of medical wires and tubes, including one on its nose, that take up about a quarter of the baby's face with the text: "Attention drug addicts and alcoholics, get birth control. Get $300. Make the call today: 888-30-CRACK."

The image on the advertisement makes it clear that it is these kinds of babies, disabled babies, which are purportedly being prevented through the project. The website also views the life of a disabled child solely as a financial drain or burden:

> The cost of hospitalization for a very low birth weight baby in need of intensive care can be as high as $150,000 or more. The annual medical cost of caring for cocaine-exposed babies nation wide has been estimated at 33 million for neonates, and as high as 1.4 billion during the babies' first year of life. (Project Prevention, 1999: n.p.)

Focusing on the cost of medical care for these disabled children reduces lives to dollar amounts and harkens back to when eugenics was in its prime. The organization intones that the lives of disabled people are too expensive for our economy and our society and, therefore, should be prevented.

Project Prevention has paid about 3,850 people to keep from reproducing through long-term birth control (2,404 people) or sterilization (1,444 people). About half of the people who have been paid by Project Prevention not to have children are from racialized groups (Project Prevention, 2011). The program has seen the sterilization or implementation of long-term birth control in drug addicts and alcoholics in every American state (Project Prevention, 2011)

In Canada, a 1986 Supreme Court decision made sterilizations without consent for non-therapeutic purposes illegal. The case that set the precedent, *E (Mrs.) vs Eve,* involved a twenty-four-year-old woman with an intellectual disability whose mother wished to have her sterilized. In this case, a lower court ruled that "the real and genuine object of the proposed sterilization was her protection. There was no overriding public interest against it" (1986: para 16). The Supreme Court overruled this decision, arguing that the intrusion on the person's civil liberties and permanent physical consequences cannot be overridden by any advantage from it. However, in the *Eve* decision, the Supreme Court left the door open to forced sterilization when it permitted non-consensual sterilization for the "treatment of a serious malady" (para. 93). While the Supreme Court set the burden high in respect to non-consensual sterilization, there are no clear guidelines as to when or under what circumstances forced sterilization of disabled people would be justified.

There are myriad cases revealing that eugenics continues to operate through legal and medical frameworks today. Take, for example, the case of Martina

Greywind, a pregnant woman charged with reckless endangerment in 1992 because she huffed paint during her pregnancy. After Greywind aborted her fetus, ensuring that a disabled baby would not be born as "a result" of her drug use, the charges against her were withdrawn (Roberts, 1997). Every time a pregnancy is intervened upon to prevent disability, eugenics is operating. Every time someone is sterilized or administered birth control against their will or without their knowledge, eugenics is operating. Eugenics is insidious and pervasive and continues to be a threat to disabled people, especially racialized disabled people and/or disabled women.

Additionally, there are more simplistic forms of controlling the reproductive capacity of disabled women than sterilization. These include the non-consensual, coerced or uninformed administration of birth control and eugenic pressures. Disabled women have been known to be administered Depo-Provera, a long-term birth control drug, without their consent (Canadian Women's Committee on Reproduction, Population and Development, 1995). These practices are a form of passive eugenics that work to appropriate women's choice and reproductive capacity in order to eliminate disabled offspring.

Further, disabled women are pressured not to have children if those children could also become disabled. In 1968, eugenicist Frederick Osborn expressed this fact:

> Perhaps the most important function of the public is to create a climate of opinion that will put pressure on carriers of defect to reduce their reproduction, and on scientists in medicine and public health to put priority on all studies that might provide leads for effective action. (97)

This pressure has been applied to many different disabled women through genetic counselling and, at times, public outcry about their pregnancies.

One example of this was the public reaction when Bree Walker, a disabled anchorwoman, became pregnant. At a time when she should have been congratulated, she was faced with national public pressure to have an abortion. People were enraged and disgusted by the fact that someone would choose to have a child that had a fifty-fifty chance of inheriting the same disability. On a radio phone-in show, one listener said Walker "had no right to become pregnant and should have an abortion" (in Kallianes and Rubenfeld, 1997: 210). Ms. Walker spoke out against the vocally disablist people pressuring her not to proceed with her pregnancy or vilifying her for getting pregnant. Walker says, "I was told by CBS management that this was a troublesome issue and that my choosing to speak out instead of just letting it go away presented a thorny issue for them" (in Cooper, n.d.a). Walker was condemned because of the eugenic values that are still held today, although they are rarely called that.

Eugenics continues to operate in the immigration system as well. While overtly racist quotas have been removed from Canadian and American immigration acts, their disablist intentions to exclude people who are "unfit" remain intact. In Canada, the *Immigration and Refugee Protection Act* (2001: s. 39 (1)(c)) states that one can be deemed inadmissible if their condition "might reasonably be expected to cause excessive demand on health or social services." In recent years, people have been excluded from entering Canada for conditions like arthritis (*Cohen v. Canada*, 2006), cerebral palsy (*Kirec v. Canada*, 2006), intellectual disabilities (*Sharma v. Canada*, 2010) and for being quadriplegic (*Alibey v. Canada*, 2004).

Immigration policies carry eugenic legacies, as do reproductive health programs in the United States. In 1968, Frederick Osborn (104) wrote, "Eugenic goals are most likely to be attained under a name other than eugenics." He went on to outline a number of eugenic achievements in postwar America, including the use of genetic counselling, which has dramatically increased since the 1960s. Eugenic organizations commonly changed their names, becoming "genetic" organizations,[11] and much of the racist, classist and disablist materials being taught in science classes before the war continued to be taught in the postwar era (see Winston et al., 2004; Paul, 1985).

Frederick Osborn, Harry Laughlin of the Eugenic Records Office and a number of other prominent eugenicists founded the Pioneer Fund in 1937. According to the Pioneer Fund's website, the organization was founded "to advance the scientific study of heredity and human differences." The organization, which continues to operate to this day, distributes grants adding up to about $1 million a year (Miller, 1994-1995) and has awarded money to a number of major colleges and universities (Pioneer Fund, n.d.b).[12] At the University of Waterloo, the Pioneer Fund has financed a current tenured professor, J. Phillipe Rushton, who has done research trying to substantiate eugenic theories that Black people have higher sex drives and smaller brains than white people (Miller, 1994–95). The Fund has also bankrolled current professor of educational psychology at the University of Delaware, Linda Gottfredson, who has put forward theories about the inferiority of Black people's intelligence (Miller 1994-95).

Conclusion

Eugenics has not disappeared; it is in our universities, in our courts, in our hospitals, at the border and on television. The eugenics model of disability lies at the foundations of how we think of disability today. Eugenics classified all people in one of two ways: fit or unfit. The entire category of unfit made up who was defined as disabled at the time. Disability, to a eugenicist, is an undesirable heritable flaw that threatens to destabilize society as a whole and should be eliminated. While eugenics often operates under other names and with less open aggression than it did in the past, it continues to function as an active consideration in a number of public policies, particularly within the medical system. As such, it is integral that we work to understand these histories, not just of the Nazi enemies who committed horrific atrocities, but of those atrocities done in our communities by our neighbours, our grandparents and even our heroes.

In understanding this past, we can recognize eugenics in our present and work to uproot it. Eugenic ideas about disability were and are formational ideas about what disability is and who is disabled.

Notes

1. Malthus did condemn aspects of society for being unjust. However, these views were largely overlooked by eugenicists.
2. Ethiopian was a term often used to describe all people of African descent.
3. While this is not the case today, at the time, homosexuals were considered to transgress the gender binary, with lesbians being considered masculine and gay men being considered feminine.
4. The British Columbian board was called the Board of Eugenics, whereas the Albertan board was called the Eugenics Board.
5. The American Birth Control League was actually renamed Planned Parenthood.
6. As a movement in North America, feminism addressed the issues and campaigned for the rights of upper-class and middle-class women. While there were poor and racialized women who fought for justice for women, they would not have been accepted or included in the first-wave feminist movement.
7. Lifton places the estimate between 200,000 and 350,000, while Biesold estimates 375,000.
8. Essondale Provincial Mental Hospital is now called Riverview Hospital. There may have been other sterilizations in other institutions or in the community, but these records are difficult to find or have been lost.
9. 70,000 sterilizations from 1900–1979 and 35,878 sterilizations from 1907–1940 (Black, 2003).
10. Excluding girls and women who had gone through menopause.
11. See next chapter.
12. These include the University of California at Berkeley and Santa Barbara, University of Calgary, University of London, University of Illinois, University of Ulster, Johns Hopkins University, University of Delaware, University of Western Ontario, University of Florence, University of Georgia, University of Texas and the University of Minnesota, Randolph-Macon Woman's College.

Chapter 3

Diagnosing People as Problems

The Medical Model

The medical model is the primary paradigm through which disability is understood within mainstream society. While eugenics was obsessed almost entirely with the eradication of disabled people, the medical model pays attention not only to the elimination or reduction of disability but also to the source of disability. The medical model evolved with the advance of modern medicine and the decline in popularity of eugenics.

The medical model posits that disability is a medical issue, a problem emerging from deviant anatomy. It is described by Steven Smith (2005: 561) as a model that "associates being disabled with fixed essential characteristics, seen via the perspective of non-disabled people and experts, that necessarily prelude a life of personal loss or 'tragedy.'" Or, in the words of Elliott and Dreer (2007: 80), the medical model is "a 'find it and fix it' perspective: health problems are diagnosed and specialized services are prescribed to cure the problem." The medical model is a clinical approach to disability which focuses on the use of diagnostic tools to identify pathology and make interventions in that pathology in order to cure or minimize it. Under this framework, disability is based in the body, normal is constructed as ideal, disabled people are dependant, and our identities are tragedies in need of intervention.

The medical model is defined and controlled by actors in the medical-industrial complex: doctors, medical researchers, pharmaceutical corporations, insurance corporations, hospitals and others involved in the medical industry. These are the experts on disability within the medical model and, consequently, on disabled bodies and minds. Autism, spinal chord injury, cerebral palsy, Down syndrome and muscular dystrophy are just some of the disabilities defined under the medical model. They are all interpreted through their medical diagnoses by medical experts.

While being the primary model used to understand and define disability, there is no single definition of disability under the medical model. For instance, *Black's Medical Dictionary* defines disability as "an observable mental or physical loss or impairment which is measurable and which may be permanent or temporary" (Marcovitch, 2010: n.p.). *The Bantam Medical Dictionary* uses "loss or restriction of functional ability or activity as a result of impairment of the body or mind" as the definition of disability (Urdang, 2004: 194). The *Miller-Keane Encyclopedia and Dictionary of Medicine, Nursing and Applied Health* (O'Toole, 2003: 524) defines disability as an "impairment of function to below the maximal level, either physically or mentally" and "anything that causes such impairment." And *Mosby's Medical Dictionary* (2006: 570) defines disability as "the loss, absence, or impairment of physical or mental fitness."

These four dictionaries all define disability differently. Specifically, *Black's* and *Mosby's* define disability as an impairment, *Bantam* interprets disability as being caused by impairment and *Miller-Keane* understands disability to be both, or either, an impairment or caused by an impairment, which is defined as a "decrease in strength or value… abnormality of, partial or complete loss of, or loss of the function of, a body part, organ or system" (O'Toole, 2003: 914). Interestingly, in defining disability in terms of the presence of an impairment "of function to below the maximal level," *Miller-Keane* defines all functionalities that are not at the highest possible level as disabilities. To complicate things further, *Black's* fails to define impairment. While the medical model has hegemonic control over the definition of disability, it does not actually uphold a universal definition of disability itself. Rather, disability shifts, even within this model, depending on social phenomena.

Medicalization

The medical model approach is expressed in rigorous and rigid scientific terms; however, it remains unable to apply a fixed definition of disability. This is likely due, in part, to the fact that, as Peter Conrad (2007: 71) points out in *The Medicalization of Society*, "there is no universally accepted definition of health." Disability is commonly perceived as a lack of health and/or functioning. These definitions are in flux. This is the case, at least in part, because what is considered disabled and/or what is considered healthy changes as social factors and norms change.

When a shift occurs in the social definition of health, new categories of disability can be created. This process is called medicalization:

> The term medicalization refers to two interrelated processes. First, certain behaviors or conditions are given medical meaning — that is, defined in terms of health and illness. Second, medical practice becomes a vehicle for eliminating or controlling problematic experiences that are defined as deviant, for the purpose of securing adherence to social norms. Medicalization can occur on various levels: conceptually, when a medical vocabulary is used to define a problem;

institutionally, when physicians legitimate a programme or a problem; or on the level of doctor-patient interaction, when actual diagnosis of a problem occurs. (Riessman, 1998: 124)

A good example of medicalization is childbirth. This was once commonly done at home and overseen by midwives, and it is now commonly done in hospitals and overseen by doctors (Van Teijlingen et al., 2004). Conrad provides further examples of recent medicalization:

Certain problems and conditions moved into the medical sphere during the previous century. These problems include mental illness, alcoholism, opiate addiction, childbirth, child abuse, and hyperactivity in children. Moreover, before the 1960s, categories such as attention-deficit/hyperactivity disorder (ADHD), post traumatic stress disorder (PTSD), anorexia, fibromyalgia, premenstrual syndrome (PMS) and Alzheimer disease were either esoteric diagnoses or not yet described in the medical literature. (2007: 118)

Menopause only began being medicalized in the 1930s (Conrad, 2007: 118). And, while the medical term for bad breath— halitosis — previously existed, it only became a commonly regarded condition with the invention, and advertising of, Listerine in the 1920s (Marchand, 1985). Both of these states of being have had medical meaning imposed upon them. Medicalization is a key component of the medical model because it is the vehicle to move something that wasn't previously considered a disability under the medical model to something that is.

Published in 1952, the first *Diagnostic and Statistical Manual* (DSM) — the book used by psychiatrists in Canada and the United States to diagnose psychiatric disabilities — contained approximately one hundred psychiatric diagnoses (Conrad, 2007). Three more editions and fifty years later, the DSM now contains about 300 conditions. As the psychiatric sphere expands outward, argues Conrad, so too does the sphere of treatment:

Problems that a decade or two ago would not have been deemed appropriate for medication are now managed with psychotropics, even apparently sometimes without any mental health diagnosis; this clearly indicates a greater implementation of medicalized solutions for human populations. (2007: 129)

This trend is likely to continue as more and more pharmaceutical medications are developed.

Another example of a recently discovered/invented medical condition is "excited delirium," which was first reported in 1982 in Seattle (Pollanen et al., 1998). According to exciteddelirium.org, excited delirium is "a brain disorder" that frequently, but not necessarily, involves the use of street drugs (excited-delirium.org, n.d.). A risk of the condition is that it may result in death while in police custody (Sullivan, 2007). Interestingly, the condition does not seem to inherently lead to death — rather, it is only fatal if the police use violent force and restraints on a captive person. Does this condition exist to describe the excited states of drug users and psychiatrized people, or is it a diagnosis used to explain the deaths of these vulnerable populations at the hands of police?

There are fundamental problems with both processes of medicalization. Diagnoses can have devastating consequences on people, leading to forced drugging, incarceration, surgeries, dehumanization, discrimination and stigma. The act of medicalizing, of establishing all or part of an individual or group as being within the medical domain, is never neutral; it is an expression of the values and needs of those with power. This power is often used to control deviance from what is considered normal. To be sure, some of this medicalization is relatively harmless, like the popularization of the diagnoses of halitosis. However, medicalization frequently brings a host of consequences onto the medicalized individual. Medicalization works to identify new categories of deviance from the norm, and as new disabilities are created and disability is individualized, the social phenomena involved in the process of medicalization are erased.

Experts, the Creation of Knowledge and the Maintenance of Oppression

The medical model does not account for systemic discrimination, or physical, social, linguistic or other barriers. Neglecting to incorporate these issues within the medical analysis actually works to perpetuate discrimination and barriers. Morsey (1988) has written of a propensity in the medical establishment that "reduces socially induced afflictions to individual-centred pathologies subject to 'cure' with the aid of scientific advanced technology" (in Filc, 2004: 1276). As such, medicine is conveniently located to decontextualize social problems and to legitimize them. This is why Zola (1972: 254), one of the bedrock theorists of disability studies, has said that "medicine is becoming a major institution of social control, nudging aside, if not incorporating, the more traditional institutions of religion and law." According to Zola, "[Medicine] is becoming the new repository of truth, the place where absolute and often final judgments are made by supposedly morally neutral and objective experts" (254).

Rather than address and change social problems that oppress disabled people, the medical model's primary function is to change oppressed individuals but leave the social structure that enables oppression intact. Under the medical model, disability is managed within the relationship between doctor (active) and patient (passive) and disability is not a social or a societal issue — it is an individual issue.

Because doctors are the experts within this model, "experts largely define disabled people's needs, and little weight is given to disabled people's own experiences" (Barnes et al., 1999: 26). Robert McRuer (2006) describes how this happens using an example from the life of Gary Fisher, a man dying of AIDS in a hospital. Fisher notified the nursing staff that there has been a mistake made by the doctors. A nurse then told him that there has been no mistake, that "errors in this profession… could be costly" (138). She also told him that he was experiencing symptoms (headaches) he was not, because those symptoms matched the (incorrect) medical judgment that had been previously made by the doctors. Because doctors, and other actors within the medical-industrial complex, are the experts, disabled peoples' experiences and knowledge are marginalized. That is, our own experiences can be disregarded or understood to be false if they contradict medical opinion.

The agents of the medical model (doctors, scientists and pharmaceutical companies) assert that their approach to disability is purely scientific. Often, they refuse to acknowledge any component of disability as socially constructed. Acknowledging that scientific knowledge is socially constructed does not dismiss science or medicine as wholly or inherently untrue, nor does it reject the need for scientific knowledge. However, it is important to recognize that scientific inquiries and conclusions are littered with social meaning and biases. Doctors authoritatively make claims about what is abnormal and what is normal, and who is disabled and who is not, based on their scientific research and their facts.

Scientific facts, however, are derived from the work of scientists, individuals who ask questions and interpret results based on their own experiences and biases. As Ruth Hubbard and Elijah Wald (1993: 6) write, "Scientists construct facts by constantly making decisions about what they will consider significant, what experiments they should pursue, and how they will describe their observations." The choices scientists make have a direct impact on the conclusions they come to. According to D. Filc (2004: 1278), this is one of the ways that "bio-medical 'facts' appear, thus, as 'things in themselves,' as 'transparent' evidence which occults their social embedding." Scientific findings frequently reflect scientists' existing worldviews, including their prejudices. According to Katrin Weigmann (2005: 301), "The more plausible a model is or the more it confirms common prejudice, the more open ears it finds, not only in the scientific community but also among non-scientists." The facts reinforce prejudices and prejudices enable the finding of fact.

The political and social roots of scientific research have been written about extensively by feminists. Ruth Bleir (1984: 3) writes, "Scientists, like everyone else, are born and raised in a particular culture of beliefs, biases, values, and opinions, and, to one degree or another, they will be affected in their work by what they hope, believe, want or need to be true." This reasoning has led biologist Ruth Hubbard (1990b: 50) to declare science "a product of human imagination." If the practitioners of medicine and other sciences accept oppressive presumptions as fact and do not question them, all of the science that stems from that research will be grounded in those underlying judgments.

Take, for example, an experience from my life: I once had a university biology professor who taught us that human beings were naturally monogamous and mated for life. There are many political and social reasons — patriarchy chief among them — why monogamy is framed as the only way to live. While I knew from my own life and the world around me that this was not true, others in my class simply accepted it as fact. As a result, in their view of the world, a view legitimized by science, anyone who was not monogamous or did not mate for life was going against human biology, going against nature.

Scientists' and doctors' knowledge is privileged within the medical model while disabled peoples' knowledge is diminished or ignored. Those of us who have been medicalized often maintain different understandings of our lives than the medical industry does. Yet they are the experts, not us. They have the power to define disability without our involvement, often completely excluding us.

Within this model, therefore, disabilities can be constructed in ways that reaffirm these non-disabled experts' beliefs about disability and disabled people. The opposing voices — those of disabled people — have already been sidelined, so an uninterrupted cycle of active marginalization which re-creates selective truths can be maintained within the medical-industrial complex. At each step, scientific knowledge reinforces the beliefs or assumptions held by non-disabled experts, and they become fact.

The Bell Curve and the Norm

Medical diagnoses are determined by the position of bodies and minds in relation to the norm. The most common tool used to assess this is the bell curve, which was named the "normal distribution curve" by Sir Francis Galton, the father of eugenics (Davis, 1995: 32). The bell curve has one central peak — the average (the normal line) — with the curve descending down and outwards in both directions from the centre. When used to chart a population, the highest point of the curve contains the largest percent of the population. The outermost edges of the curve — closest to zero — contain the fewest number of people, the people furthest from the norm.

Originally an astronomy tool, Galton applied this method of charting averages to general statistics and divided the curve into quadrants. Eugenicists were interested in increasing the genetic, physical and intellectual traits of the people who fell within the third and, particularly, the fourth quadrants of the curve (these people were considered to be above or better than the norm). Through selective breeding, Galton wished to eliminate those who fell within the first quadrant, those who were the farthest below the norm.

Of course, no matter who makes up a population, there will always be people who fall within each quadrant. If every disabled person were eliminated, the curve would adjust and there would be a new group of people who populated quadrant one, a new group of people who would be below average and would be considered disabled. Lennard J. Davis (1995: 29) calls this curve "a symbol of the tyranny of the norm."

Nonetheless, modern medicine frequently uses the normal curve as a diagnostic tool. Conditions that are considered physical disabilities are frequently defined solely in terms of the absence of normality. Little people — people with the medical diagnosis of dwarfism — are by definition small compared to the average human height. The generally accepted, yet highly arbitrary, height for people diagnosed with dwarfism is 4 feet 10 inches (Adelson, 2005). However, individuals who are members of ethnic groups that have a low average height are generally excluded from the 4-foot, 10-inch cutoff. Therefore, dwarfism is based not only on the average height, but it is also expressly linked to the cultural groups and communities one is a member of.

Shortness, other than what is diagnosed as dwarfism, has also been medicalized. Extreme shortness (the bottom 3 percent of heights for a particular age group and gender) is called idiopathic short stature (ISS). There is a human growth hormone (HGH) that is used on the shortest 1.2 percent of children with ISS (Conrad, 2007). As Harlan Lane (2008: 279) argues, "Shortness became a disability, once a treatment was available." Shortness was not a medical condition until medication could be prescribed to treat it (Conrad, 2007; Lane 2008). Children with ISS may be considered disabled under the medical model because their height causes physical limitations and/or social exclusion, yet the heights of children who are considered extremely short have risen over the past century. If HGH had been available at the beginning of the twentieth century, it would not have been used on children of the height that it is being used on now. Put another way, the heights of children considered to be extremely short, and thus treated with HGH, are increasing.

Similarly, obesity — now considered a disability — is a relatively recent medical and social concern. Riessman (1998: 136) argues, "Weight is also a good example of medicalization because it illustrates in a most graphic form how power relations are maintained through medical social control." A hundred years ago, the medical industry was primarily concerned with people being underweight, not fat (Czerniawski, 2007). Obesity was classified as being 20 percent above the average (rich, white person's) weight for many years (Maine, 2000). This classification still exists, but medical opinion has largely shifted in favour of the body mass index (BMI), which has an arbitrary classification for establishing obesity and uses standards that remain based on the "ideal" body weight (Czerniawski, 2007). Views of weight have changed so much that an ideal weight in the early 1940s is considered overweight today (Jutel, 2011). In 1998, the American government chose to re-scale the BMI. As Margo Maine (2000: 35) writes, "Without gaining a pound, millions of Americans, whose BMI's were considered normal on the 16th, woke up the next day to learn that they were in the danger zone." Thousands upon thousands of people were suddenly considered at risk of being obese[1] because of a change in political and medical definitions. Conrad (2007: 119) argues, "In the past two decades, at least, we have seen the medicalization of obesity; that is obesity is viewed not just as a risk factor for medical problems … but as a disease in itself."

Using the medical model, a number of courts have found that obese people are disabled, ruling that "obesity can, on a case-by-case basis, be found to be a disability" (*McKay-Panos v. Air Canada*, 2006: para 34), and "obesity itself can constitute an impairment" (*State Div. of Human Rights ex rel. McDermott v. Xerox Corp*, 1985). It is also the position of the United States government's Equal Employment Opportunity Commission that if one is obese it is "*clearly an impairment*" (emphasis original, in Henry, 2007). Though the Supreme Court of Canada has not addressed obesity as a disability directly, it has found that "both an ailment, even one with no resulting functional limitation, as well as the perception of such an ailment" can be considered a disability (called a handicap by the Court) (*Quebec v. Montreal v. Boisbriand*, 2000: para 24). As obesity is clearly considered an ailment, under the medical model it would also be considered a disability. However, a number of court cases in both the United States and Canada have found that obesity is not a disability (see Henry, 2007; Luther, 2010). While the medical industry presents obesity as a clear and scientific category today, this category has shifted based on society's changing political and moral values rather than on "pure" science or in the interest of public health.

The norm, or average, is used commonly to define psychiatric and intellectual disability as well. The American Psychiatric Association (APA) defines mental retardation (intellectual disability) as someone having an IQ score of seventy or below (APA, 2000). IQ tests are scored so that the mean score will be one hundred, so, intellectual disability is directly related to the norm because anyone with a score of 70 percent or less of the average will be considered retarded. The APA goes on to describe mental retardation as "significantly subaverage general intellectual functioning." Stuttering ("Disturbance in the normal fluency and time patterning of speech"), anorexia nervosa ("refusal to maintain a minimally normal body weight") and primary sleep disorders ("endogenous abnormalities in sleep-wake generating or timing mechanisms") are also psychiatric diagnoses, or disabilities, that are overtly defined as being in opposition to the norm.

Medical Gaze

Once something or someone has been medicalized, the medical gaze then becomes the filter that is applied to medicalized peoples' experiences. The medical gaze is necessarily a non-disabled gaze looking at the disabled body. Disabled people's primary diagnoses become the singular point through which all other information about them is viewed. It is through the medical gaze that the doctors saw Gary Fisher as having headaches when he did not. It is through the medical gaze that, according to Griffin Epstein (2011), a front-line service provider at a drop-in centre for psychiatrized people saw an individual with schizophrenia locked in a psychiatric ward for days instead of being treated for a kidney infection. Indeed, one study found that psychiatrized people's "requests for further examination and referrals to specialists were generally ignored and their physical health concerns were attributed to their mental illness" (McCabe and Leas, 2008: 310). Doctors are more likely to down-play a physical complaint by someone with a psychiatric history, and they are less likely to order tests for that person (Garber et al., 2000).

Because our lives and experiences are interpreted through the medical gaze, they are limited to what the medical industry has defined as biological and physiological. It means that if you are fat, you are medicalized, and this has many consequences on your life. As Doctor Keith Bachman reports, "Someone will see a provider for foot pain, and all they hear is, 'Lose weight. It will get better.'" (in Rowen, 2008: 8). Bariatric researcher Kelli Friedman says, "Often, I hear that my patients will go into their physician complaining of some health ailment. The doctor will blame almost everything wrong with them on their weight. While weight may or may not be contributing to the health problem, the patient walks away feeling that's all the physician focused on" (Rowen, 2008: 8). There is also evidence to show that fat people are much less likely to be given preventative screening tests than thin people (Rowen, 2008). Doctors also have less respect for fat people (Huizinga et al., 2009). While a thin person with a medical concern may be treated respectfully, examined, medicated or given further tests by a doctor, a fat person may have the same concern attributed to their weight.

My most profound personal experience of being subject to the medical gaze happened in my early twenties. I got very, very sick; my symptoms progressively worsened. I stopped being able to eat most of the time, I started fainting and had intense abdominal pain all the time, but my doctors attributed these symptoms to my primary diagnosis — the diagnosis that I had that put me under the rubric of disability. Even symptoms that did not match my diagnosis at all were interpreted as being caused by my primary diagnosis. As a result, I spent two years getting increasingly sick. I had cancer, a tumor in my kidney that was not fully or properly investigated. Had I not already been disabled, I would have been treated very differently and much more thoroughly. This is what medicalization and, specifically, the medical gaze, does to people's lives.[2]

The filtering of people's experiences through their diagnoses can have intense implications for people who are disabled. This is not to say that every person who has been labelled as disabled experiences the demeaning, minimizing and disregarding consequences of the medical gaze every time they go to the doctor. This filtering, however, is a trademark of the medical model that has real, sometimes devastating implications on the lives of disabled people. Experts continuously tell us what our experiences are, and our identities, in thier view, revolve around our diagnoses. This is one of the ways the medical model is able to retain a tight control on the identities and lives of disabled people.

Medicine as Control

All disabled people have moral and economic judgments imposed upon them as part of the disability labelling process, but these are particularly apparent in the scientific discipline of psychiatry. Definitions of psychiatric illnesses have been identified, added, revised and deleted from psychiatric texts time and time again. These shifts are based on the needs of those in power, and the definitions have been used as tools for social control. For instance, Dr. Michael Greger explains that, while slavery was widely practised in the United States, many slaves were diagnosed with "drapetomania." This psychiatric disease was described as "'an irrestrainable propensity to run away.' For slaves with drapetomania … a simple procedure — amputation of the toes — was used" (Greger, 1999: Appendix 43). This diagnosis was used to legitimize both slavery and the torture of individual slaves through a medical identification of disability.

Many defiant or deviant groups have been targeted for social control by the medical/psychiatric profession and labelled as disabled. Don Weitz, a psychiatric survivor and longtime activist, argues that the psychiatrist's largest weapon for labelling and marginalizing individuals is the DSM:

> Psychiatrists manufacture hundreds of "mental disorders" classified in

its bible titled Diagnostic and Statistical Manual of Mental Disorders (DSM). The DSM is not a scientific work but a catalogue of negative moral judgments which psychiatrists use to medicalize, target and stigmatize dissidents and alternative ways of perceiving, interpreting or being in the world. (1988: 159)

Psychiatrists make political and moral decisions about specific kinds of people and use the DSM as a reference tool to justify this. Women (Chesler, 2005: Ehrenreich and English, 1976), homosexuals (Marcus, 1992), vegetarians (Greger, 1999), masturbators (Silverstein, 2008), people on social assistance (Jarrett, 1921) and many others have been targeted by psychiatrists and/or diagnosed with psychiatric conditions and labelled as disabled because of their identities or actions, all of which are considered medically normal today. Disability is not a neutral category within the medical model, it is politically loaded and used to identify and stigmatize people and behaviours that are considered abnormal or morally wrong.

These moral and political judgments affect people beginning at birth and continue on throughout their lives. For instance, medicine is deeply invested in upholding the social belief that there are only two sexes: male and female. Babies born with genitalia that challenge this belief are pathologized and targeted for medical intervention (Kessler, 1998). Doctors perform surgeries and other interventions on intersexed babies because they do not fit into contemporary views of the world. According to M. Morgan Holmes (2008: 169), author of a number of texts about intersexuality, there is a "medical presupposition that intersex characteristics are inherently disabling to social viability." So, people are changed to match the prevailing worldview, rather than the view being changed to include people who don't fit.

There are numerous examples of how medicine has used the disability label as a tool for social control. Genetics is becoming a moral battleground where social phenomena are ignored and social issues are targeted as disabilities. The inferiority (read: disability) of Black people and women was "proven" by scientific study at one point in time (Bethlehem, 1985); however, as political views shifted, so to did the disability label. As the economic and social needs of mainstream society change, those changes are reflected in the medical model's formulation of disability.

The Medical Model's Implications on Disabled Lives

The medical-industrial complex, using the medical model of disability, has massive amounts of control over our lives. It legitimizes control with stories of how medical practitioners are the experts on us: our bodies, our minds and what we need. This control can be exerted at any time, even on a daily basis. Michelle Dawson, an autistic woman who studies the impacts of medicalization on autistic people, illustrates the pervasive nature of the medical-industrial complex:

> What happens in research will have a big effect on your life; on how you live, on decisions made about you by other people and so on. And, when you are autistic you have no say in this at all. What happens in research is you have this wide array of non-autistic people who are making all these decisions according to their needs, their abilities, their parties, their goals. (in *Quirks and Quarks*, 2006: n.p.)

This is the case not only for autistic people but for everyone who experiences medicalization, and it is reflected, in varying degrees, in the lives of disabled people and the policies that impact us.

Take, for example, Little Ashley X, a nine-year-old disabled girl whose life was forever changed because of the power of doctors over disabled people's lives. In Seattle, in 2004, Ashley X had a hysterectomy and her breast buds removed. These surgeries were performed primarily for the purposes of keeping Ashley small, but her breast buds were removed to keep her from being sexualized. She was also put on estrogen so that she would remain small. This was all done so her parents could continue to lift her. Her parents obtained the operation, which would result in her sterilization and permanently stunted growth, saying they wanted to "improve our daughter's quality of life" (in Liao et al., 2007: 16). Practically none of the media reports on this case showed any coverage of the many lifting devices available to disabled people, as well as the other possibilities available to the parents, including the hiring of attendant care. Instead, doctors attempted to chemically and surgically desexualize Ashley and keep her small because Ashley was devalued, and her parents' interests were prioritized over her own. The surgeries performed on her have been dubbed "the Ashley Treatment" (Lao et al., 2007) and may be used in the future against other disabled girls.

Once someone has been classified as disabled under the medical model, it can impact any or every aspect of that person's life. The medical model has largely been institutionalized and entrenched by governments — in fact, the model is widely used to allocate resources and define rights. Social assistance legislation commonly uses the medical definition of disability to determine eligibility. Take the Ontario Disability Support Program and the Supplemental Security Income (USA) for example. These programs variously define disability in terms of a person's ability to perform particular kinds of activities. Both require the disability to be permanent, or to last at least one year, and require medical documentation. The *Ontario Disability Support Program Act (ODSPA)*

(2001: 4. (1)(b)) defines disability as being unable to perform one of the "activities of daily living." These activities include working, participating in the community and personal care. Supplemental Security Income (ssi) (Social Security Online, 2010) defines disabled as a "marked and severe functional limitation." The medical model is used to determine if disabled people can access these benefits, and doctors make individual determinations for the state.

In addition to controlling access to social assistance, doctors have an unimaginable amount of control over other areas of disabled people's lives. They have the power to allocate resources to disabled people by providing medical information that is translated into non-medical resources. Doctors are typically not trained to deliver social services. Yet, doctors can control the distribution of everything from accessible housing and transportation, workplace accommodations, mobility aids, attendant care, training and education, technology, counselling, income and food. These are not necessarily, or even remotely, medical resources, and it would be preposterous to imagine medical providers having control over many of these essentials for non-disabled people.

Doctors, who get paid about seventeen times more than a single person receiving ODSP, rarely have an understanding of what it is actually like to live in poverty.[3] This class bias can lead to a skewed understanding of the importance and necessity of these resources. In my work with the Ontario Coalition Against Poverty, I have had discussions with a number of health care providers and their patients about a benefit called the "Special Diet." This benefit allows between $10 and $250 per person, depending on their health conditions, and requires a form to be filled out by a medical provider in order to qualify. Many doctors will not bother to fill out people's forms to give them access to small amounts of extra money per month. Yet, that money may make an important difference in the life of someone on social assistance, who, by definition, does not have food security. Many doctors don't understand the value of $10 for poor people often because they have never lived in poverty.

There is a strong dynamic within the medical model of disabled people both being held in contempt by doctors for our deviant bodies, minds and actions, and being under their control to be "saved" from ourselves. This means that disabled people are often put in precarious and vulnerable positions that often lead to abuse. Because doctors have the power to imprison, many disabled people are relegated to institutions, including nursing homes, psychiatric institutions, prisons and hospitals, when they could live in the community. In *No Pity*, Joe Shaprio (1993: 300) argues that institutions "evolved from the model of a prison, not a home, so there was tacit license to disrespect the 'inmates.'" Institutions are used to house disabled people, particularly those with intellectual disabilities, psychiatric diagnoses and cerebral palsy. Institutions, argues John O'Brein in his article "Out of the Institution Trap" (2005: 64), are used as a way to "impose segregation and supervision on people who require accommodation and assistance due to impairments... treating them as if they were devalued or dangerous or disgusting to 'others.'" In other words, institutions become a place to permanently storehouse the disabled. Thus, many disabled people are punished for their disabilities and denied basic personal freedoms because the medical industry individualizes disability and views it as something that should be contained and profited from if it cannot be eliminated.

Institutions are hotbeds of abuse. About a quarter of psychiatrized inpatients in Ontario are subjected to physical or chemical restraints or seclusion, even though this type of treatment "is intended to be a method of last resort," according to the Canadian Institute for Mental Health Information (2011). Some of the more extreme examples include a Florida man with a brain injury who was allegedly tied to a bed by institutional staff for two and a half years (Wells, 1998). Horror stories of food deprivation (Nursing Standard, 2006) and torture (Wells, 1998) have also been uncovered. As well, rape is "an everyday reality" for some women in psychiatric institutions, according to anti-psychiatry activists Bonnie Burstow and Don Weitz (1988: 26).

Electroshock, Incarceration, Experimentation and Medical Killings

Psychiatric facilities have a history of being laboratories for human experimentation. During the 1950s and 1960s, experiments were performed on about a hundred people at the Allan Memorial Institute in Montreal, Quebec. There, according to Burstow and Weitz (1988: 28), they "were forcibly subjected to an unprecedented combination of psychiatric tortures; regressive electroshock, massive drugging, sensory isolation, prolonged sleep therapy and psychic driving." These CIA funded experiments also administered psychedelics (LSD) and hallucinogens (PCP) to people and subjected them to insulin-induced comas as well as electric shocks (Klein, 2007).

During and prior to this period, psychiatrists also frequently used experimental surgery on individuals. The lobotomy, a surgery that caused permanent brain damage, was the most common. Dr. Thomas Szasz (2007: 152) argues that the "claim that lobotomy causes brain damage is tautological: lobotomy is the surgical destruction of healthy brain tissue." The lobotomy is a form of psychosurgery that entails cutting into the frontal lobe with the aim of eliminating a psychiatric condition. This was the first time that doctors could make alterations specifically to the brain to treat psychiatric conditions (Braslow, 1997). Lobotomies were considered successful, even though the procedure turned people "docile, apathetic, indifferent" (146). The cure that lobotomy provided was actually the control of people by horrifically altering their person-ality. People of all ages had the surgery performed on them, including children (Dully and Fleming, 2007). By the end of 1949, about 10,000 people had been lobotomized (Kolb, 1953), and, two years later, about 20,000 people had had the surgery in the United States (Braslow, 1997). Shortly thereafter, however, lobotomy largely fell out of favour. Today, there are still some psychosurgeries performed, but they are not lobotomies per se (Ellis, Abrams and Abrams, 2009). The primary medical interventions used today are no longer surgical, due to the development of new medications and the increasing popularity of electro-convulsive therapy (ECT).

Many psychiatric institutions are part of a medical industry that continues to experiment with electroshock "treatments." ECT was developed in 1938 by an Italian psychiatrist (*Quirks and Quarks*, 2008) and was being used by a third of psychiatrists by 1966 (Shorter, 1997). While it has been in use for seventy years and is the "treatment of choice for major depression," according to medical historian Dr. Edward Shorter (1997: 208), doctors still don't understand why ECT, supposedly, works. Shorter, one of the biggest proponents of ECT and author of *A History of Psychiatry: From the Era of the Asylum to the Age of Prozac*, admits, "In ways that are still a little bit mysterious it reestablishes the normal electrical currents of the brain. There is something about that convulsion that is therapeutic and what exactly it is isn't yet understood" (*Quirks and Quarks*, 2008). Electroshock can be excruciatingly painful, causing memory loss as well as substantial changes in personality.

ECT zaps over a hundred volts of electricity into the brain for thirty to sixty seconds (*Quirks and Quarks, 2008*). ECT has been used on people with a number of psychiatric diagnoses, the most common being depression, bipolar disorder and schizophrenia (*Quirks and Quarks, 2008*), but, ECT has also been used on individuals diagnosed with postpartum depression, alcoholism, anxiety (No Force Coalition, 2000), anorexia nervosa, weight or appetite loss, neurotic disorders, narcotic addiction, obsessive-compulsive behaviour, sleep disturbance, retardation, morbid guilt and delusion (Baldwin and Jones, 1998). This list may soon include autism (*Quirks and Quarks*, 2008).

While not fully understood, about 15,000 Canadians and 100,000 Americans are subjected to ECT every year (Hoag, 2008; Dahl, 2008).[4] The use of ECT is incredibly widespread, and its use is justified with the claim that it saves lives. However, in a comprehensive literature review of ECT studies, John Read and Richard Bentall found that the number of deaths caused by or during ECT is far higher than official estimates:

> There is no evidence at all that the treatment has any benefit for anyone beyond the duration of treatment, or that it prevents suicide. The

> very short-term benefit gained by a small minority cannot justify the
> significant risks to which all ECT recipients are exposed. (2010: 344)

Read and Bentall conclude that ECT has been largely overhyped and that there
has been a widespread failure on the part of researchers to properly study ECT
using placebo controls.

The medical establishment is one of the biggest, if not the biggest, perpe-
trators of abuse against disabled people. Beyond the institutional abuses and
use of ECT, disabled bodies were also experimented on without consent for
over half a century.[5] In the 1950s, the polio vaccine was tested on a number
of intellectually disabled children in several institutions. One of these tests
resulted in the death of one-quarter of the children, while half were paralyzed
(Smith, 2009). Following World War II, U.S. government scientists injected
plutonium into eighteen people, who were (wrongly) thought to be dying, to
see what the consequences would be. The youngest person injected was five
years old (McNeill, 1993). Over one hundred children in a Massachusetts
institution were fed Quaker Oats laced with radiation in nutrition experiments
in the mid-twentieth century (O'Neil, 2001). Intellectually disabled children
in New York's Willowbrook State School were purposely fed feces infected
with hepatitis between 1956 and 1970. The purpose of the experiment was to
infect the children in order to help doctors find a vaccine (Paola et al., 2010).

The resulting deaths of patients who received ECT were far from exceptional. Whether or not the aim is to gather scientific information, doctors have
been known to kill a number of disabled people. The Holocaust is an infamous
example of medical murders, but disabled people have been killed in Canada
and the United States as well. Because disabled people are seen as less valuable
within the medical model, the withholding of treatment and other ways of
killing people are seen as less wrong or not wrong at all.

In 1973, doctors Raymond Duff and A.G.M. Campbell published "Moral
and Ethical Dilemmas in the Special-Care Nursery" in the *New England Journal
of Medicine*. In this text, they document how they withheld lifesaving treatment
from forty-three newborns. Duff and Campbell wrote, "To escape 'wrongful
life,' a fate rated as worse than death, seemed right" (1997: 65). They made the
claim that life with a disability is not worth living.

Similarly, in 1977, Anthony Shaw concocted a formula to rate the quality
of life of a disabled newborn and, thereby, determine whether or not the child
should be allowed to live (Shaw, 1988). The formula was $QL = NE \times (H+S)$,
where "QL is quality of life, NE represents the patient's natural endowment,
both physical and intellectual, H is the contribution from home and family,
and S is the contribution from society" (Gross et al., 1983, 456). Therefore, a
baby's quality of life is directly related to the class of the parents if the "natural

endowment" is not determined to be zero. If the family was poor, their child would have a far smaller quality of life rating and a far greater chance of being killed. As Shaw (1988: 11) asserts, "Quality of life, while not the only legitimate criterion (longevity and cost would be others), is not only relevant but central to humane medical decision making."

Shaw's forumula was used in the justification of a study involving the denial of medical treatment to thirty-three babies diagnosed with spina bifida between 1977 and 1982 at the University of Oklahoma Health Sciences Center (Gross et al., 1983). These babies were supposed to be kept "comfortable" until they died. Ultimately, five of the thirty-three children were later given medical treatment because their parents demanded it. Three of the children lived and were doing well at the time the final report on the program was written (Gross et al., 1983: 452).

The view of these doctors was that it was better to be dead than to live a disabled life. A 1997 study examining deaths in intensive care nursery units resulting from withdrawal or withholding of treatment found that in over half of the cases involving infants quality of life concerns were documented (Wall and Partridge, 1997). Almost a quarter (23 percent) of all deaths involving the withdrawal of medical support listed quality of life concerns as the only reason for the death (Wall and Partridge, 1997). This means that in 23 percent of cases where treatment is withdrawn, the infants' deaths occur because doctors (and possibly family members) don't think that their disabled lives are worth living. When doctors rate quality of life, however, they frequently rate it lower than disabled people do themselves (Gill, 2000; Saigal et al., 1999; Gerhart et al., 1994). Medical students also have more negative views of disabled people than the general population does (Tervo et al., 2002). As the medical model depicts disability as an individual medical issue, often one worse than death, killing disabled people can be seen as an act of pity or charity.

What's Wrong with Disability?

What is so wrong about just "curing" all disabled people anyway?[6] A presumption made about disabled people is that we all aspire for normality. People like Christopher Reeve and Rick Hansen are given extensive media coverage in their quest for the cure. However, those disabled people who do not want a cure and are happy with their bodies are ignored. Many disabled people like all or part of the things that earn them disabled labels, and many disabled people are proud to be so and would not choose to change. Carol Gill (1994: 46), a disabled psychologist, wrote of her frustration with non-disabled people's "need for us to be non-disabled" and with people who "either wish I could be normal or who need to see my disability as an unimportant part of me."

Our disabled identities are important to many of us. While I am in incredible pain at times, I value the things that I get from my body — a body that is considered disabled. I appreciate my slow, laboured walk because I notice things that many other people don't. My pain and my inability to do certain things also makes me very efficient, skilled at delegation and thoughtful about help and asking for it. These are parts of my personality that I am proud of and couldn't imagine living in the world without. I couldn't imagine not being disabled. It is not an accessory; it is an inseparable part of me.

Many disabled people do not want to be cured. Ari Ne'erman, an autistic person appointed by President Obama to the National Council on Disability, advocates that we stop "trying to make autistic people something we are not and never can be: normal. This focus on a cure has prevented us from actually helping people." Ne'erman says, "We need to stop making autism advocacy about trying to create a world where there aren't any autistic people" (in Silberman, 2010). Likewise, ABILITY magazine editor-in-chief Chet Cooper (n.d.b) says, "There are many people with spinal cord injuries that live a fully functional quality life, independent of walking and don't feel their injury is something that needs to be cured." These narratives are almost always missing from the discussion about the medical model and the quest for the cure. Curing or eradicating disability is simply impossible. Bodies, minds, actions and ways of being are identified as disabilities because of their distance from the norm. There will always be differences between people; there will always be bodies, minds, actions and ways of being that are the furthest from the norm. Therefore, there will always be disability.[7]

Despite the impossibility of curing or eliminating disability, the focus of the medical establishment remains fixed on eliminating certain kinds of people rather than oppressive social conditions. The medical industry has put massive resources into reducing smoking and obesity, both of which increase the likelihood of fair or poor (rather than good or excellent) health, by 53 and 74 percent, respectively (Raphael, 2007).[8] Poverty, on the other hand, increases the likelihood of having fair or poor health by 307 percent (Raphael, 2007). Even though poverty is the single most significant determinant of health in Canada (Raphael, 2007), doctors aren't telling us that we need to cure capitalism. Globally, war and poverty are the greatest causes of impairment (Oliver, 2009). How many doctors are researching how to prevent war or poverty? How many are writing prescriptions for peace or money? While so many people in the world are poor, and while disabled people and our organizations have been arguing for accommodation and acceptance, resources continue to be funnelled into the effort for "the cure."

Preventing Disability Before Disability Starts: Prenatal Screening

Many resources are directed towards prenatal screening in order to try and eliminate disabilities (or disabled fetuses) in the womb. In Canada, with a public health care system,[9] prenatal testing is a routine part of medical care for many pregnant women. In the United States, where health care is a luxury item for many people, prenatal testing is less frequent but still commonplace. Tom Shakespeare (1998: 675) describes prenatal screening as "like a roller-coaster, where testing may take place without the knowledge of the pregnant woman or where testing is presented as a routine procedure." While prenatal testing is frequently discussed in the context of "choice," Shakespeare (675) concludes that "women are not encouraged to exercise choice and control, and place considerable trust in the expertise of their advisors."

Eugenicist Frederick Osborn writes how genetic counselling is underpinned by eugenic ideology:

> Heredity clinics are the first eugenic proposals that have been adopted in a practical form and accepted by the public.... The word eugenics is not associated with them. The couples who go to them for advice are interested in not having an abnormal child, rather than in the less personal goal of improving the race.... Reports from these clinics indicate that couples are considerably influenced by the information they receive in the clinics, and generally, but not always, they are influenced in a eugenic direction. (1968: 91)

By 1951, the United States had ten heredity or genetic clinics (Kevels, 1985); today, there are over 1,100 genetic clinics and 350 genetic laboratories (National Center for Biotechnology Information n.d.a; n.d.b). In Canada, there are at least 80 genetic counselling clinics (Canadian Association of Genetic Counselors. n.d.).[10]

Abortion rates following a prenatal diagnosis for Down syndrome are 85 to 95 percent or more (Schechtman et al., 2002; Mansfield et al., 1999; Hassed et al., 1993), 95 percent for cystic fibrosis (Harmon, 2004) and 81 percent for aneuploidy (abnormal number of chromosomes) (Shaffer et al., 2006). In Canada, abortion rates of disabled fetuses increased 578 percent between 1991 and 1998 (Liu et al., 2002). In Europe, meanwhile, one Danish headline is telling: "Plans to make Denmark a Down syndrome-free perfect society" by 2030 (Somerville, 2011). Of course, the associating a lack of Down syndrome with societal perfection is both terrifying and utterly false.

Additionally, testing is far from flawless. In regards to testing for neural tube defects (spina bifida and similar conditions), the majority of positive test results are in fact false positives — they indicate the presence of a defect, which is absent upon further testing. Overall, about 5 percent of women get positive results for neural tube defects and require further testing (Hubbard, 1990a).

Critiquing prenatal testing is not equivalent to saying that women should not have abortions. Women who want or need abortions should have easy and free access to them, like they should have to all forms of health care. However, it is troubling that women are expected to make eugenic, "socially minded" choices when faced with defect-positive prenatal test results. It is also problematic that disabled people are not provided with adequate support and resources, such that women feel even greater social and financial pressure not to have disabled children. As Ruth Hubbard (1990a: 118) said, "Focusing the discussion on individualistic questions, such as every woman's right to bear healthy children (which in some people's minds quickly translates into her duty not to 'burden society' with unhealthy ones) ... obscures crucial questions." These questions are ultimately about how we distribute resources, structure our society and place value on people.

A study of genetic researchers, many who have been studying genetics for more than ten years, revealed that 82 percent supported the abortion of fetuses that would be "severely mentally retarded," as opposed to the 76 percent who supported an abortion if the child would definitely die from its condition at or before age four. Many also supported abortion for lifelong obesity (12 percent), depression (11 percent), homosexuality (7 percent) and the undesired sex (5 percent) (Rabino, 2003: 376). It is these people, with these values, who are designing and implementing genetic tests and working to eradicate many disabilities

Sex selection of fetuses has been occurring since 1986, according to feminist author Patricia Spallone (1989). Some female fetuses are given the same treatment as many disabled fetuses are — they are aborted because they are not seen as having any significant value. There have been proposals to use in vitro fertilization (IVF) sex selection to eliminate the possibility of carriers of X chromosome-linked genetic diseases (Spallone, 1989). Spallone (145) calls this proposal "a most presumptuous eugenic tactic, defining us as fit to live according to our reproductive capacity and quality of our genes."

Those who are directly impacted by prenatal screening, and who supposedly benefit from it, would be much better served if the resources allocated to screening were injected into social programs that worked to meet basic needs of disabled people and reduce the barriers they face. Prenatal testing is a gross misapplication of resources. According to Ruth Hubbard and Elija Wald (1999: 35), "Population-wide screening to detect unsuspecting carriers [of cystic fibrosis] would cost more than one million dollars for each child who might otherwise develop the condition." Screening would cost $5 million for every case of spinal muscular atrophy (SMA) (Little et al., 2010) and $0.6 million for every case of fragile X syndrome (Musci and Caughey, 2005). Population screening for SMA was not recommended because it was not considered to be cost effective (Little et al., 2010). However, it was recommended for fragile X syndrome, the most common cause of genetic intellectual disability, because it would save roughly $34,102 for every prevented birth (Thomas et al., 2005). While these are American studies, when screening programs are implemented in Canada, assuming costs similar to those in the U.S., the public health care system spends hundreds of thousands, even millions, of dollars to prevent the birth of a single disabled person.

Further, the costs that are measured in cost-benefit analyses are priced in a disablist world. For instance, the SMA study factored in the cost of home renovation to make the home physically accessible for a disabled child (Little et al., 2010). If there weren't physical, social and structural barriers for disabled people (barriers that could be reduced with the diversion of screening funds), these costs would be dramatically reduced, even eliminated, in some cases.

Even by genetic evolutionary logic it does not make sense to eliminate specific genes and specific populations of disabled people without fully understanding the genetic implications. It is generally accepted that genes exist for a reason. Genes that have remained in a population are generally considered to have had some significant use. For example, carrier genes for sickle-cell anemia result in a stronger resistance to malaria, while cystic fibrosis is believed to provide some resistance to tuberculosis (Moalen and Price, 2007). Type-1 diabetes provides resistance to hypothermia, and hemochromatosis, a genetic iron deficiency, is believed to help resist the plague (Moalen and Price, 2007). Dick Sobsey, a disability researcher, argues, "placing a negative value on these [conditions] without understanding their natural role may be extremely dangerous" (Canadian Press, 1998). Working to eliminate human genetic diversity means that we are working to eliminate the diversity that could ultimately help protect the human race from pandemic viruses, bacteria or devastating environmental changes.

Medical providers now have a legal responsibility to seek out what they consider to be fetal defects and notify pregnant women if a so-called defect is found. Doctors can be sued for misinterpreting test results or failing to notify a pregnant woman of a potential health condition in her unborn child. Likewise, genetic counsellors can be sued for "wrongful birth" for failing to advise prospective parents of the "genetic risks" of having a child. Fertility clinics can also be sued if the resulting child is disabled (*Health Law Litigation Reporter*, 2003). These lawsuits, according to *Liddington v. Burns* (1995, n.p.), are not about medical practitioners causing "injury or harm to the child, but ... whether that defendant's negligence was the proximate cause of the parents being deprived of the option of avoiding a conception," or making a choice "to terminate the pregnancy" (*Liddington v. Burns, 1995*). Similarly, the Supreme Court of Alabama ruled against medical professionals when a disabled child was born, stating that "the parents of a genetically or congenitally defective child may maintain an action for its wrongful birth... [when a medical practitioner fails]... to discover and inform them of the existence of fetal defects" (*Keel v. Banach*, 1993: n.p.). In other words, one could launch this type of lawsuit when a disabled child is born because the presumption is that disabled children should not necessarily be born and that medical practitioners have a duty to prevent these births.

In Canada, these lawsuits appear to be less common. However, a British Columbia judge did order a doctor to pay one couple who had a child with Down syndrome $200,000 because they did not learn about the diagnosis in advance. This doctor's so-called negligence prevented the mother from accessing an abortion, which she would have done had she known about the diagnosis (Blackwell, 2003).

Some courts have raised alarm bells about the eugenic nature of these types of lawsuits. One American court ruled in *Taylor v. Kurapati* (1999: n.p.), "The very phrase 'wrongful birth' suggests that the birth of a disabled child was wrong and should have been prevented." The judge went on to say that if it was found "that the birth of one 'defective' child should have been prevented," it could also be argued that "the births of classes of 'defective' children should similarly be prevented, not just for the benefit of the parents but also for the benefit of society as a whole through the protection of the 'public welfare.' This is the operating principle of eugenics." The court, in *Grubbs v. Barbourville Family Health Center* (2003: n.p.), also warned that these kinds of lawsuits could be used punitively for not enacting eugenic practices by "identifying and eliminating any disabled children in the womb."

While these suits are used against practitioners within the medical industry, they use the medical model to give the legitimacy and ultimately work to reinforce the idea that disability is about flawed individuals, deviant bodies and tragedies that should be prevented at all costs. Of course, these costs include the complete undervaluing of disabled people's lives and self-worth as well as, in many cases, their feelings of being desired and loved by their parents.

Eugenics Inside the Medical Model

Wrongful life and wrongful birth litigation is one of many places where the lines are blurry or non-existent between the medical model and eugenic model.

Prenatal testing has obvious eugenic implications, as can doctor assisted suicide. This is not simply a case of overlapping schools of thought, however. Eugenics formed the basis of genetics, and much of contemporary genetic science began as eugenic science.

There are numerous examples of simple name changes in scientific journals and organizations where "eugenics" was replaced with "genetics" or another authoritative scientific word. For instance, the *Annals of Eugenics* became the *Annals of Human Genetics* (Watt, 1998; Black 2003),[11] the *Eugenic News* became the *Biological Science* (Thom and Jennings, 1996), the Eugenics Society became the Galton Foundation (Thom and Jennings, 1996), and the *Eugenical News* became the *Journal of Social Biology* (Black, 2003).[12] Other eugenic organizations re-branded themselves to gain legitimacy through genetics, such as the American Breeders' Association, which changed its name to the American Genetics Association (Troyer and Stoehr, 2003; Black, 2003), and the Human Betterment League of North Carolina, which became the Human Genetics League of North Carolina (Black, 2003).

The Minnesota Eugenics Society became stagnant in the 1930s, but following the Society's founder Dr. Charles Fremont Dight's death in 1938, the Dight Institute for the Promotion of Human Genetics was established at the University of Minnesota (Minnesota Historical Society, n.d.). Sheldon Reed, head of the Dight Institute, coined the term "genetic counseling" as he felt "genetic hygiene" (modelled after the German phrase "racial hygiene") sounded like a toiletry (Li, 2000). When the Eugenic Record Office at Cold Spring Harbor Laboratory closed, its files were given to the Dight Institute (Black, 2003). Cold Spring Harbor Laboratory is now an important genetic research facility (Wilson, 2002). As Edwin Black (2003: xvii) argues, "American eugenic institutions rushed to change their names from eugenics to genetics. With its new identity, the remnant eugenics movement reinvented itself and helped establish the modern, enlightened human genetic revolution."

Where there was no name change, there was still a foundation in eugenics for many genetic organizations and publications. All of the founding editors of *Genetics*, a scientific journal founded in 1916, were proponents of eugenics (Beckwith, 1993). This journal continues to operate today. A number of genetics textbooks contained eugenics material (Beckwith, 1993). For example, Edmund Sinnott and L.C. Dunn (1925: 406) wrote in the *Principles of Genetics* that "even under the most favorable surroundings there would still be a great many individuals who are always on the borderline of self-supporting existence and whose contribution to society is so small that the elimination of their stock would be beneficial."

These kinds of eugenic mentalities existed long after World War II. In his

1971 presidential address to the American Association for the Advancement of Science, geneticist Bentley Glass declared that "no parents will in that future time have a right to burden society with a malformed or a mentally incompetent child" (in Rowland, 1992: 116). Eugenics didn't vanish, it became embedded in components of the medical model, and how that model defines and relates to disability is heavily influenced by its eugenic roots.

Many personal traits and behaviours have been attributed to genetics in part or entirely. These components of human diversity are being, have been or could be marked as disabilities and targeted for elimination. Such behaviours include: shyness, religiosity (Beckwith, 1993), conformity, creativity (Mahwald, 2000), novelty-seeking (Matthews et at, 2003; Mahwald, 2000) and mental weakness (Horsburgh et al., 2009), as well as polygamy, criminality (Wilson, 2002), addiction (Mahwald, 2000) and overeating (Zastrow and Kirst-Ashaman, 2010). Perhaps most dangerously, genetics has been used to explain oppression. Genes have been attributed to xenophobia, male dominance, (Beckwith, 1993) and men raping women (Thornhill and Palmer, 2000; Badinter, 1992). Some white scientists use genetics to try to legitimize racism, arguing that Black people are inherently less intelligent (see Rushton and Jensen, 2010; Alland et al., 1996; Rushton, 1995). Like eugenicists, actors within the medical-industrial complex seek to label undesirable people as disabled and unwanted personalities or behaviours as disabilities.

Conclusion

Whether or not the medical model manifests itself in eugenic ways, it remains highly problematic. This model establishes certain kinds of bodies and behaviours, and certain kinds of people, as acceptable or deviant and seeks to eliminate those that do not fit within its classifications of normal. These classifications are created with little or no consultation with those of us who are considered disabled because we are not considered to be the experts about our own lives. The consequences for falling outside of the norm can be devastating: institutionalization, abuse, poverty, loss of autonomy, dehumanization and eradication.

The medical model individualizes disability, roots it in the body and seeks to cure or reduce it. Some of the consequences of the medical model for disabled people have been the erasure of the oppressive factors leading to the labelling and maintaining of disability, a minimization or marginalization of our own knowledge about our experiences, the inability to access appropriate medical care, abuse, confinement and even death. The medical model has acted as an oppressive force on the lives of disabled people; this is why many disabled people are calling for its elimination.

Rejecting the medical model, however, does not necessitate a rejection of medicine or medical care. It would constitute a rejection of the "tyranny of the norm" (Davis, 1995: 29) and require the economic incentives and industry-growth elements of the expansion of medical diagnoses and interventions to be scrutinized. Imagine what the world would be like if the resources that were devoted to eliminating disabled people were devoted to assisting disabled people and building strong communities. Imagine what medicine would look like if neither medicalization nor the medical gaze existed. There has to be a way to provide care without demonizing disability and, therefore, disabled people. Only by working to undo the medical model and by replacing it with disability models that focus on social justice and come from the bottom up — from disabled and other marginalized people — will we ever be able to achieve these changes.

Notes

1. "Obese" is the medical term I generally use when discussing fatness in the medical context. However, fat has largely been reclaimed by fat people, and I feel that it is, generally, a more respectful word.
2. To be fair, some of this was likely related to homophobia, transphobia, sexism, ageism and classism, rather than solely attributable to the medical gaze.
3. Average Ontario doctor's salary: $213,000 a year (Canadian Press, 2006). Basic ODSP cheque, as of December 2009: $1,053 a month (Income Support Advocacy Centre, 2010).
4. The Canadian number is based on incomplete information, so it is likely higher (Hoag, 2008).
5. Of course, disabled people are not the only group of people who have been targeted for non-consensual human experimentation. For example, the Tuskegee syphilis experiments between 1932 and 1972 involved the study of hundreds of Black men with syphilis. The doctors monitoring them never told them that they had syphilis, nor did they offer any of the known treatments for the disease. As a result, the disease was needlessly spread (Reverby, 2009).
6. Of course, not all cures are the same. Curing arthritis or spinal cord injuries or autism or schizophrenia or cancer are all very different things. Some of these things are always considered disabilities, others are sometimes considered disabilities. The common criticisms of "finding the cure" for other illnesses, diseases and disabilities largely does not apply to cancer because cancer is often a terminal illness. You cannot accommodate cancer (although you can accommodate many of its symptoms). However, curing cancer involves another set of problems. As a cancer survivor, I am terrified of curing cancer as finding a cure does not address the environmental and social conditions which I believe are responsible for the rise in cancer rates. A cure would simply allow us to continue to maintain our unhealthy and polluting societies without making the changes that both people and the planet desperately need.
7. The majority of disabilities are acquired, primarily, because of war, poverty,

accidents and infections. While poverty and war can and should be eliminated, there will always be things that happen that shift normal people into the range of abnormal.

8. Just because fat people are more likely to have poor health does not mean that obesity leads to poor health. Fat people are treated worse by doctors, which leads to fewer tests and specialist referrals, which could mean that minor issues become major ones before they are dealt with.

9. This is not actually universal health care, as migrants without immigration status, those in Canada as temporary workers and some students do not receive health care.

10. All numbers are counted from clinic lists on websites.

11. First, it became subtitled as "A journal devoted to the study of human populations," which was then changed to "A journal of human genetics." The full title of the journal changed in 1945.

12. In 1954, it became *Eugenics Quarterly* before becoming *Social Biology* in 1969. *Social Biology* continues to publish today.

Chapter 4

For Us, Not with Us

The Charity Model

Like the two models already discussed, the charity model is based on the notion of inequality between those who are identified as disabled and those who are not. This framework accepts and reinforces the medical model (and, at times, the eugenic model), particularly, the notion that disability is located in individual minds and bodies and that it can and, where possible, should be cured. Like the previous models, the charity model is an understanding of disability developed by people who are not disabled themselves but have tremendous power and resources and act in their own interests when constructing and employing this model.

In the Middle Ages, the Christian formulation of disability was established for the purposes of bestowing charity. Disabled people were considered the "deserving poor" and received alms where others, including the children of the disabled, were denied charity or forced to do work in order to receive it (Stiker, 1999). In the fifteenth and sixteenth centuries, disabled people played a very important role in society. In *Crooks and Paupers,* Bronislaw Geremek writes: "When they are not able-bodied and are incapable of work ... they offer the rich the possibility of acting on their charitable feelings and thus win salvation" (in Stiker, 1999: 84). So, charity bestowed on the disabled was a relatively quick and simple way for the rich to insure access to heaven.

However, during this period, who was considered disabled was not necessarily rooted in people's bodies or minds. In *A History of Disability,* Henri-Jacques Stiker (1999: 84) argues that the lines between disability and marginality were "problematic to distinguish." Many people who would be considered to have intellectual disabilities today would not have been considered disabled during the Middle Ages (Gleeson, 1999). Classifications of disability were not clear or exact and were closely linked to people's capacity to work. Charity was limited to people who were unable to work due to a perceived physical, intellectual or psychiatric abnormality. Stiker (1999, 87), observing the Middle-Age Christian model of divine intervention, writes, "God sends us disease and disability as trials on the one hand, as opportunities to exercise our greatest virtue, charity, on the other, and thirdly as the sign of his presence." Disability, both useful and necessary, was as much, or more, about the person acting on the disabled body — the charitable person — as it was about the disabled person.

During the eugenic period, charity was often discouraged because of the Malthusian belief that it would breed poverty and misery. With the decline of eugenics, however, the charity model regained its influence. The charity model is an authoritative paradigm today through which much of the imagery of disability is created. The charity model often accepts and reinforces medical model definitions of disability, but it adds a moral element to its understanding of disability. This model does not only base disabilities in individual bodies, it often presents those bodies as innocent victims of the tragic disabilities that they bear.

Today, the idea that it is better to give than to receive remains a common assertion in the Western world. The charity paradigm constructs a notion of disability for the benefit of the giver, not for the disabled recipient. Additionally, charity works to construct social notions about disability by invoking images and ideas of disability and producing disabled recipients as the other. This is often complementary to and informed by the medical (and occasionally eugenic) model. Like the medical model, the charity model has an industry dedicated to upholding and expanding it. Indeed, the actor in the charity model of disability is the charity industry itself, not disabled people. Charities may fail to improve or may negatively interfere in disabled people's lives in essentially two ways: through the allocation of resources and through the construction of disabled people's identities as individual and tragic, rather than social and positive.

Charities: Big Money

Rather than advocating for change, the charity model and the charity industry are typically invested in the status quo. As disability is an individual tragedy, solutions are based on eliminating or reducing disability rather than addressing social barriers. Disability charities are big business. American charity revenues run into the billions, if not trillions of dollars a year (see Table 1). In Canada, with a much smaller population, disability related charities are still very lucrative (see Table 2). Thirteen of the twenty-five highest paid executives of charities in the United States in 2009 were from disability or health-related charities (American Institute of Philanthropy, 2010).

The approach to disability taken by the majority of these organizations portrays the lives of disabled people as tragic and asks people to end their "suffering" by donating spare change or pledging money to find a cure. These organizations are innumerable, and many are familiar household names. According to Eli Clare (1999, 104), these groups support the quest for the

Table 1: American National Chapter Charity Revenues, 2009/2010[1]

Charity	Revenue (US$ in millions)
American Cancer Society	$903.2
Easter Seals	$750.2
Cystic Fibrosis Foundation	$313.3
March of Dimes	$212.1
Muscular Dystrophy Association	$190.8
National Alliance for Research on Schizophrenia and Depression (NARSAD)	$20.0

Table 2: Canadian National Chapter Charity Revenues, 2008/2009 or 2009/2010[2]

Charity	Revenue (CA$ in millions)
Canadian Cancer Society	$220.2
Ontario March of Dimes	$97.6
Cystic Fibrosis Canada[3]	$13.8
Easter Seals	$4.0
Schizophrenia Society of Canada[4]	$0.8

cure "to the exclusion of supporting independent living and civil rights for disabled people."

Charity industry money rarely goes to helping to make our lives better. While some charities may spend money on wheelchairs, assistive devices and other supports that people need, most charities do very little to meaningfully improve the lives of disabled people. By and large, disabled people live in poverty while billions of dollars are funnelled into the charity system every year. These funds are generally not used to provide housing, food, attendant care, health care or assistance devices to disabled people. Rather, the money largely goes to prevent the existence of future disabled people.

The majority of the charities acting on behalf of disabled people are not led by disabled people. If they were, the funds they raise would likely be used in very different ways. Not only is "finding the cure" an offensive and wasteful endeavour for charities to pursue, but many disabled people do not want to be cured.

Charities' first priorities are often themselves, and they spend large percentages of their revenue on fundraising and research, rather than direct support. The Canadian Cancer Society put 41 percent of its expenditures into fundraising, 30 percent into research and prevention and only 16 percent into support programs for people living with cancer (Canadian Cancer Society, 2010). Cystic Fibrosis Canada put 45 percent of every dollar raised into research, 13 percent to administration, 10 percent to fundraising and 19 percent to clinics and patient services (Cystic Fibrosis Canada, 2010). It appears that no money goes to support people living with cystic fibrosis outside of medical services. The Schizophrenia Society of Canada (ssc) puts 22 percent of every dollar spent into human resources and administration and 14 percent into fundraising (Schizophrenia Society of Canada, 2008–2009). No money raised by the ssc goes to support people diagnosed with schizophrenia; however, 5 percent goes to advocacy which includes advocating for, among other things, employment, housing and "access to newer medications" (Schizophrenia Society of Canada, 2008–2009: 2). According to Muscular Dystrophy Canada's 2010 annual report, the organization spends 47 percent of the money it brings in on fundraising, 15 percent on research, 12 percent on operations and 24 percent on services for disabled people (Muscular Dystrophy Canada, 2010). These numbers, however, are somewhat misleading because 34 percent of all of Muscular Dystrophy Canada's revenue goes to compensation for staff (Canada Revenue Agency, 2011),[5] which would be interspersed throughout their other expenditures. All of these charities clearly prioritize themselves and/or research (i.e., trying to get rid of disabled people) over supporting disabled people.

The Ontario March of Dimes is the only disability charity I have researched that actually spends a great deal of its revenue on services for disabled people. The organization only spends 4 percent of its revenue on fundraising, and roughly 89 percent goes to support for disabled people.[6] Much of these resources, no doubt, go to pay the Ontario March of Dimes' 1,577 employees (Ontario March of Dimes, 2009–2010). This particular charity, unlike its American counterpart, says that it "turned its mission from 'cure' to 'care" decades ago (2).

The simple fact that much of the funds raised by the Ontario March of Dimes goes to programming for disabled people, which is incredibly rare, does not mean that the charity is acting to benefit disabled people. There are critics of the Ontario March of Dimes programs. Anne Abbott is a disabled artist, activist and blogger involved with cross-disability organization DAMN and its anti-attendant-care abuse campaign. Abbott has friends who have used Ontario March of Dimes independent living programs. "The March of Dimes may be the best at allotting funds for people with disabilities and programs but programs like their attendant care are run so badly" she says, that they can be "abusive" (2011). Abbott argues, "It's the type of care that they give that is awful." She includes disablist attitudes, paternalism, arbitrary restrictions, poor staff training, lack of privacy, refusal to learn to communicate with some of the people they are providing services for and threats of institutionalization if someone complains as some of the problems with the programs. Independent living services make up roughly 43 percent of Ontario March of Dimes' expenditures (Ontario March of Dimes, 2009–2010). The organization asserts: "Satisfaction with service remains high at 85%" (8).

The March of Dimes in the United States spends 37 percent of its revenue on public and professional education (March of Dimes Foundation, 2010), which largely focuses on eliminating disabled people. Its "project to reduce birth defects" has produced a video that says, "Babies born to overweight or obese moms have an increased risk of birth defects. This is something that we would love to see women be able to prevent" (March of Dimes, n.d.). This so-called public education implores women to take up a eugenic responsibility to help ensure that disabled children are not brought into the world.

Another video produced by March of Dimes also has eugenic undertones. Done in the format of a reality show about getting women to eat well and exercise, *Don't You Dare* refers to the main character, a woman in her twenties, as "Mama" even though she has no children. It demonstrates the importance of vitamins, exercise and healthy eating on health and repeatedly stresses reproductive health. It tells the audience: "All women our age should take a multi-vitamin... make sure there is 400 micrograms of folic acid" (March of Dimes, 2007). This dosage of folic acid is recommended for women because it will prevent certain disabilities in a fetus if a woman gets pregnant, not because it is a necessary dosage for women (Public Health Agency of Canada, 2008). This subtly eugenic propaganda piece, done in the name of "public education," uses disability charity dollars to pressure women to prevent disabled children.

Charity and Corporations

Within the charity framework, the overarching economic system is not problematized, but rather the individual's capacity to function within that system is. As such, capitalism is not problematic; indeed, the charity model provides space for a softer side of capitalism. The Christian notion of salvation for the rich through charity has been modernized through corporate use of charity to simultaneously soften the blows of capitalism and grant economic salvation through increased market share and tax breaks.

Corporate donations have become a mainstay on the charity circuit, particularly with the famed telethon. The most renowned telethon, which began in 1952 with host Jerry Lewis, is for the Muscular Dystrophy Association (MDA) (Longmore, 2005). In 1966 Jerry Lewis and the MDA telethon went national (Longmore, 2005). These day-long spectacles — part variety show, part commercial — are incredibly expensive undertakings: the 2009 MDA telethon cost over $19.3 million to produce and brought in $45.6 million, making expenses 42 percent of total revenue (MDA, 2009b). The story of the MDA telethon, a telethon that I watched many times in my youth, remains relatively similar from year to year. Jerry Lewis tells some jokes, musicians, dancers and other acts perform, and in between we hear of the tragedy that is muscular dystrophy. Some of this we are told by the host, but some we are shown through the sad eyes of the children who are trotted out. Across the telethon stage, we are told about these children, their sad lives, the hopes that they have that may never be realized and how they might die terribly young.

Corporate CEOs come out periodically to announce how much money they have raised, giving them a chance to appear as down-to-earth, regular folks. These moments are great public relations opportunities for corporations, but in reality the companies frequently don't actually raise the money themselves. Each time someone makes a donation and signs a shamrock or paper egg for Shamrocks Against Dystrophy or the Paper Egg for Easter Seals campaign, or every time a worker wears jeans for the United Way, the money gets paid to the corporation as a donation. Then, the corporation takes credit for that donation. Paul K. Longmore, a disabled historian who has extensively researched the charity industry, writes about this process:

> Telethons could show that big companies cared about little people. Businesses of all sizes, but especially large corporations, could identify themselves with worthy causes, community needs and family values. They could link themselves in the public mind to those positive concepts by generating donations from their customers and employees and then offering the donations to those companies. (2005: n.p.)

As such, the corporation (rather than disabled communities) benefits substantially from charity donations.

When businesses participate in charity drives they can generate new customers because people come into the store to donate. Local newspapers run articles that are free publicity. A *Regina Leader Post* article informs readers they can "Buy an Egg to Help Send a Kid to Camp" by buying "their paper eggs for $1 each from its national supporters, Money Mart and The Bargain! Shop, and from its regional sponsors like Peavey Mart, SARCAN Recycling Centres, Mac's Convenience Stores and the Conexus Credit Union" (Benjoe, 2010: A5). Or, when consumers go to the till, they may be asked if they would like to make a donation (usually between one dollar and five dollars) for a specific charity. As customers make their purchases, they may feel good because the corporation is supporting charity, which increases their positive feelings about that company. Canada Safeway practises this for a number of disability charities: Muscular Dystrophy Canada, Easter Seals, Prostate Cancer Canada, the Canadian Breast Cancer Foundation and the Special Olympics (Bascaramurty, 2010). While Canada Safeway gets to take credit for raising millions (about $6 million all together), it only actually donates about 7 percent of that amount (Bascaramurty, 2010).

Cause-related marketing, or charity work, has become, in the words of P. Rajan Varadarajan and Anil Menon (1988: 60), "a way for a company to do well by doing good." This is why corporations put so much effort into telling consumers about all the charity work that they do. In fact, the amount that a corporation spends on advertising telling people it is giving to charity can even exceed the amount that it actually donates to charity. Unfortunately, records of advertising expenditures are difficult to obtain, but there are a few examples. General Mills spent $7 million in advertising and coupon printing to inform its customers that it donated $1 million to the MDA (Finger, 1987). Philip Morris extensively advertised its charitable contributions, some of which went to fight hunger for people with AIDS in 1999 (Muhammad, 1999). The tobacco company donated $60 to $75 million to charities and spent $100 million advertising its contributions (Cone et al., 2003; Stole, 2008). In 2006 a number of corporations including Apple, Motorola and Gap launched project Red. Each corporation would donate a percentage of the sales of particular red products to the Global Fund to Fight Aids, Tuberculosis and Malaria; these percentages varied from about 8 percent to 50 percent (Stole, 2008). About a year after the project had been launched, Mya Frazier (2007), writing in *Advertising Age*, reported that Red had only raised $18 million, but its main corporate licensees had spent as much as $100 million on advertising. Red argued that the report was false and that the corporations had only spent twice as much on advertising ($50 million) than they had raised ($25 million) (Nixon, 2008). No matter what, advertising the good work of these corporations far outstripped what they actually donated. All of these corporations acted not out of the goodness of their hearts in participating in cause-related marketing schemes, but out of the pursuit of growing profits.

Seeking exposure and increased sales is why some companies have bought, through sponsorship, the names of charity fundraisers like the CIBC Run for the Cure, the American Airlines Celebrity Ski for the Cystic Fibrosis Foundation, the Scotiabank AIDS Walk for Life and the Avon Walk for Breast Cancer. Charity support has become a business strategy. As marketing consultant Carol Cone put it, "Now, the question about charity is, can it support corporate business?" (in King, 2001: 115).

The money that businesses can make from charity has become a marketing strategy, both for those businesses and for the charities themselves. Budweiser encouraged bars to get involved with its charity fundraising, assuring them that "nothing beats the volume or the profit you'll enjoy with the Bud family of beers. So talk to your distributor about shamrocking for MDA and get ready to roll in the green" (in Longmore, 2005: n.p.). The Canadian Cancer Society heralds the "Bottom-line benefits" of giving to the organization with such catch phrases as "Enhance your corporate image," "Build brand value," "Increase sales" and "Stand apart from the competition" (Canadian Cancer Society, 2011).

Charities also act as public relations vehicles to soften corporations' images to the public. Charitable contributions or campaigns to support disability-related charities can help heal damaged public images when corporations have received bad publicity. Kirk Davidson (2003) documented how the alcohol industry gives large sums of money to disability charities. He argues that this is an intentional ploy to transfer blame away from the physical and social damage that alcohol can cause. Additionally, Sears Canada was a corporate sponsor of Children's Cancer Charities while it had five hundred workers locked out of a warehouse (United Steel Workers, 2010). American Airlines, which received $7.1 million in fines in 2008 for safety and other violations and experienced increased FAA oversight following three landing incidents (Prada and Pasztor, 2008), was an "Outstanding Corporate Partner" for the Cystic Fibrosis Foundation and a member of the Susan G. Komen for the Cure (for breast cancer) "Million Dollar Council Elite." Roche, a pharmaceutical corporation and one of *Multinational Monitor's* "10 Worst Corporations of 2008" for withholding AIDS medications from poor people and countries that attempted to cap the price (Weissman, 2008), sponsored camps for disabled children as well as the international Roche Walk for Children. The Bank of America received a $20 billion bailout and had $100 billion protected losses in 2009 (Rucker and Stempel, 2009) while it guaranteed a minimum of $1.95 million and a maximum of $2.7 million to Komen for the Cure.

Each of the above corporations has been accused of doing awful things such as mistreating workers, damaging the economy, endangering safety and endangering lives, and each gives money to disability-related charities with the intention and effect of improving its public image. Inger Stole (2008: 21) argues, "The practice of cause marketing suggests that businesses may leverage the existence of dire social problems to improve their public images and profits while distracting attention from their connections as to why these social problems continue to exist." Corporations participate in causing social problems then exploit those problems as marketing opportunities.

Disability-related charities not only assist corporations in creating the illusion of "good work," they also work to help uphold the capitalist system itself. Charities help to lighten the blows of capitalism by redistributing some resources, apparently in the direction of "correcting" society's shortfalls. While charities support those who are the so-called deserving poor, the tacit assertion is that the "undeserving" poor are without assistance by their own fault. That is to say, they are not victims of an unjust capitalist system.

Thus, corporations, charities, medical researchers, accountants, performers and telethon hosts all benefit from this arrangement. Whether or not disabled people benefit is not particularly important within the charity paradigm. Because the charity model is more about the giver than the receiver, corporations also give consumers the opportunity to be givers and to feel good without actually having to do something that they would not have otherwise done. Berglind and Nakata (2005: 452) suggest that this type of marketing is "substituting consumption for morality." Additionally, marketing professor Michal Strahilevitz writes how the charity paradigm assuages the guilt of the consumer:

> By linking small donations to the purchase of products, marketers can give consumers an opportunity to feel good about making a contribution, without feeling bad that they are not giving more. Indeed, because the amount to be donated is determined by the seller of the product rather than by the buyer, the consumer is not likely to feel accountable for the amount contributed, only for the fact that a charity-linked product has been purchased. (1999: 218)

Therefore, one can feel the joy of giving even when, in reality, one may have given as low as 0.05 percent of the profits from that product (Strahilevitz, 1999) (which could amount to less than a penny) to charity. Indeed, almost all consumers, including accountants, over-estimate the amount of the donation when it is presented as a percentage of the profits from a product (Olsen et al., 2003). Further, some of these types of marketing campaigns are intentionally misleading (Olsen et al., 2003).

Many corporations profit in concrete and quantifiable terms from their attachment to a charity. Research shows that product (and, specifically luxury product) sales and market share increase if a donation is given to a charity (Strahilevitz, 1999; Barone et al., 2000; Pracejus and Olsen, 2004). A corporation can increase both its sales and its profits if it donates even a small, inconsequential percentage of profits to charity. Along with the profit increase, a corporation can then attend a telethon or run ads and boast to a national or international audience about the supposed good work it has done, simultaneously receiving free publicity and, depending on the type of donation, a tax credit.

Disabled People: The "Product" of Charity

The product that disability, medical and health charities peddle is disabled people. In order to create the most marketable product, charities construct disabled people in three important ways: as children, as white and as objects to be pitied. As an experiment, think for a moment about the advertisements for disability organizations that you have seen or heard. Now try to remember how many of them did not involve white children. I conducted an informal study of hundreds of advertisements for charities and almost all of them prominently featured white children.

The child is an important advertising tool for charities — some of them even have official "poster children." They sell the image of helping "innocent victims" and the potential future of promise rather than suffering. The story goes like this: the child depicted could be an astronaut or an athlete if only they could be given the cure that you, the consumer, could make possible. A pair of advertisements by the Huntington Society of Canada illustrates this cliché. One features a photograph of a girl in a ballerina outfit, while the other shows a boy in an orange jumpsuit holding a rocket. Both children are standing in the front of the classroom, as if at show-and-tell. The chalkboard above the first child reads, "When I grow up, my mind and body will slowly deteriorate until I choke to death trying to swallow," and the other says, "When I grow up, I will be wracked by spasms so severe, I'll burn 5,000 calories a day" (Huntington Society of Canada, n.d.).[7] Below each photo is the website and phone number for the organization, both include "cure HD" (Huntington's Disease). Children, unlike disabled adults, do not have spoiled futures. Children are not perceived as economic drains on society; rather, they are potential contributors whose economic identities as productive citizens can be realized.

These advertisements tell us of the necessity to protect children's future aspirations or simply to protect their futures. The Cystic Fibrosis Foundation has mastered the use of children in its propaganda. One ad shows a blond seven-year-old boy. Above him are the words of Broc Glover, an accomplished motocross racer and the child's father: "Some parents dream about their kids growing up to be motorcycle champions. I just dream about my son getting a chance to grow up." The next text, from the cute, sad boy reads, "Please help my dad find a cure" (Broc Glover's Breathe Easy Ride Against Cystic Fibrosis, 2009: n.p.). The consumer is implored to make a donation to help this adorable, innocent child have a future. The ad does not mention that most kids with cystic fibrosis do grow up to become adults, with the mean age being 37.4 years old (Medline Plus, n.d.).

Children are even used in charity promotions for diseases that they do not typically experience first-hand. For example, a CIBC Run for the Cure pamphlet depicts seven white girls in private school uniforms with a pink ribbon wrapped around them. The text below the image reads: "We're running for the future." These children compel us to save them by making a donation, even though they may never personally know someone who is affected by breast cancer. If consumers are not saving children from their dangerous futures, they are saving them from their families. The MetLife Foundation says in one of their advertisements that "you'd be surprised how early the effects of Alzheimer's can set in." Below this text, and the close-up photo of a child, we are informed that Alzheimer's disease "steals normal life from caregivers, spouses, children and grandchildren alike" (in *Ad Punch*, 2007: n.p.).

While disabled people are frequently represented as children, they are perhaps more commonly depicted as white. When there are people of colour in photographs, they are almost always in groups that also include white people. Racialized communities in Canada and the United States are labelled as disabled disproportionately compared to white people (Raphael, 2007; Emmett, 2006). Further, the vast majority of disabled people (75 to 80 percent) live in the Global South (*New Internationalist*, 2005; Parens et al., 2009). Yet the image portrayed by the charity industry is very much that of the North American white disabled person. Why? The first obvious answer is racism, which pervades all sectors of society. The kind of racism at play here has a particular economic incentive; charity advertisements are about maximizing fundraising through the construction of a white disabled person, whom white people will more likely pity, as a ploy to generate more money. The under-representation of racialized people in charity advertising corresponds to the under-representation of the same groups in advertising generally. People of colour are rarely portrayed in commercial advertising, and when they are they are usually not alone or the primary character (Entman, 2006). The absence of racialized people in advertising reflects the systemic racial bias of the media.

Of course, some racialized people are the central focus of charity advertising. For example, a Multiple Sclerosis Society ad in Britain from the late 1990s depicts a Black man on his knees with his body stretched over them, hands open and resting on the floor. The man has the arm of a white person around him, supporting him. The text of the advertisement reads: "Multiple Sclerosis is still incurable. Without us, it always will be" (in Barnett and Hammond, 1999: 311). Thus, the representation of racialized disabled people reinforces and strengthens a strange hybrid of an "ethic of care" intertwined with the idea of the "white man's burden" of the last century, where white people named themselves the saviours of racialized people and better able to rule their societies than the indigenous inhabitants themselves. This representation is also closely linked with interventionist politics at the international level, where Western imperialism is guided by the principles of "aid" and "keeping the peace." Through this ad, whiteness and ability are understood as integral to the survival of racialized disabled people.

Generalized racism in the media manifests in particularly troubling ways with respect to charity advertising. While North American charities for North American children almost always use young, white children, there are charities that exclusively depict Black children in their advertising. You have seen these ads: small Black children with wide, vacant eyes and distended bellies, sometimes with flies on them, sometimes in bed staring at the camera. These children, disabled because of their hunger and lack of health care (or, sometimes, because of landmines) implore the (white) North American viewer to give their pity and money. These children, argues Akua Benjamin (2005: n.p.), are "overwhelmingly presented not ... as sweet, cheerful and brave," like the brave white disabled children for charities in North America. Rather, they are depicted as "overwhelmingly destitute, overwhelmingly needy... and so they are presented in terms of a trope, about deserving the charity of whites, deserving of charity or pity of us living in the North, deserving our charitable good will." This depiction of disability is very different than that of the white disabled child, whose innocence and purity is on the forefront, rather than her "savagery."

Pity is marketed to us at the expense of the many complexities that exist about disability and the many truths that define what it means to be disabled. Pity is sold to us because pity sells better (Eayrs et al., 1994). For example, when protestors criticized the MDA's representation of disabled people as pitiful, spokesperson Jerry Lewis said, "If it's pity, we'll get some money. Pity? You don't want to be pitied for being a cripple in a wheelchair? Stay in your house!" (in Nelson, 2003: 177).

In order to sell us tragedy, the charity industry constructs visual cues about what it looks like to have an intellectual or psychiatric disability label. The "look," or the construction of the physical traits of intellectual and psychiatric disability, is necessary in order to evoke emotional responses (pity and sadness) in consumers. As such, both groups have a number of similarities: sad eyes with vacant stares, scruffy hair and a dishevelled general appearance. These people are usually photographed alone.

Intellectual disabilities, however, have an additional physicality when presented in charity advertising. Some genetic conditions, such as Down syndrome, do have physical characteristics that correspond with them. Yet, there is no definitive way to tell by looking whether a person has an intellectual disability. Charity advertising, however, has constructed the idea of what intellectual disability looks like for marketing purposes. Caroline Eayrs and Nick

Ellis (1990) found that a number of charity advertisements "relied either on the characteristic features of Down syndrome or rather vacant-looking people photographed in an unsympathetic way" (in Doddington et al., 1994: 244). While this study is quite old, it would appear that the same visual clichés are still relied upon by the charity industry.

In three recent advertisements for the Special Olympics, advertising agency Grey Group Canada shows a single white person in each ad. Two of the people in the ads, a young man and a young woman, appear to have Down syndrome; the older man in the third ad does not. These three people all look unhappy and are staring vacantly at the camera. These images are overlit and are not full of the dark shadows common in advertisements depicting intellectually disabled people. The photos are unflattering and look like they could be mug shots, driver's licence photos or pictures out of a medical textbook. Each ad depicts an individual's head and torso in two images. The image on the left shows the person from the front and the image on the right shows the person from the back. All three people are similarly posed with similar white t-shirts on. The ad with the young man is wearing a t-shirt that says, "Think I'm Slow?" on the front. The back of his shirt says, "Let's Race." The other two people are wearing similarly messaged t-shirts. At the bottom of each ad, in very small print, it says, "Help support Special Olympics and give people with intellectual disabilities the confidence to win at life" (Grey Group Canada, n.d.).

The positive messaging of the ads is overwhelmed by the imagery and makes up only a tiny fraction of the ads (less than 10 percent). Advertisements like these are some of the ways that charities have constructed a visually identifiable intellectually disabled person who is instantly recognizable as an object of pity.

"Overcoming" Disability, Supercrips and the Abled-Disabled

Occasionally, what at first glance appears to be the opposite of a pity object becomes a marketable representation of disability: the "supercrip."[8] Supercrips are also called the abled-disabled. Tanya Titchkosky writes:

> The abled-disabled are those people who can exclude attending to disability by attending fully to their ability to participate in society, as normally as is possible, and they ultimately and inevitably signify having a "positive effect on others," "contributing fully to the community," and "maximizing their potential".... The stories of the abled-disabled demonstrate that even disabled people are able to fit in and take up an appearance which shows that their conduct is undoubtedly oriented to an unquestioned normalcy. Through this way of conceptualizing

> disability, disability becomes the space in which the value of normal shines forth without ever having to be directly spoken of, and disabled people are held to be asserting their individual ability (value) when they can be seen as oriented to serving this normal order. (2003: 530)

Supercrips are not necessarily special for their actions; rather, they are special because of the emotional response or the feeling of inspiration they can elicit in others.

Often, supercrips do nothing special at all. Instead, writes disabled activist Eli Clare (1999: 8), "These stories rely upon the perception that disability and achievement contradict each other and that any disabled person who overcomes this contradiction is heroic." Everyone knows the characteristics of the super-crip: determined, motivated and, above all, inspirational. As disabled historian Paul K. Longmore (2003: 231) reminds us, "We have all seen it incarnated by disabled heroes on television, those plucky overcomers who supposedly inspire us with their refusal to let their disabilities limit them."

Supercrips are inspirational because they do normal things. Like millions of people, and most children, supercrips play childhood sports. Adam Bender played a number of sports on his crutches, making him one of *People* magazine's "Bravest Kids." The magazine also said that nine-year-old Adam had "courage to spare" because he played sports (Fowler et al., 2008: 82). Disabled people are exceptional for being employed, like Bill Porter who has cerebral palsy and lived as an "unsuspecting hero" because he took on the job of a door-to-door salesman (Brady, 2002:1). Disabled people are gutsy when they dance like amputee Heather Mills. Upon her first appearance on *Dancing with the Stars*, she was called an "inspiration" by one judge and was told, "you've got more guts than Rambo" by another (CBC News, 2007).

When *Time* magazine wrote about an extraordinary couple — they both have black belts in martial arts, one plays multiple instruments and the other is a public speaker — one might think that their eclectic achievements would be the story. Instead, the story's *raison d'être* was the remarkable fact that they both had Down syndrome and they were getting married. The fact that these two disabled people found someone else to love them was the reason for the article and their supercripdom (Walls, 2006).

Of course, sometimes it is actually the extraordinary achievements of people that garners them their supercrip status. Rick Hansen, who pushed his wheelchair across thirty-four countries (or, about 40,000 km), in his Man in Motion World Tour in order to raise money to find a cure for spinal cord injuries, is an example of this type of supercrip (Rick Hansen Foundation: n.d.). While Hansen, like Terry Fox, Franklin D. Roosevelt and many others, worked very hard for this status, it remains out of their control. Supercrip status — whether it is granted because you get married, have a job, play sports, wheel around the world or become president — can be revoked at any time if those with power so choose. Further, while it would appear that supercrips are the only disabled people who do not evoke pity, this is not actually the case. The supercrip is constructed on top of pity. These "achievers" are useful not because they have achieved, but because they have done so in spite of their disabilities. Supercrips are not inherently inspirational; they are inspirational because they are objects of pity, though that pity is transformed into inspiration.

Charities help construct the supercrip to promise us what is possible if we simply make a donation. They show people overcoming their disabilities and send the message that disabled people can achieve with your donation. Tori Boyles is a young, white girl featured in an Easter Seals video.[9] The video shows a girl who has come leaps and bounds from doctors' prognoses. According to one Easter Seals staff person, "You can't envision what she was like seven years ago." Tori is presented as a determined, sweet child who, in the words of her mother, "never gives up." She is a supercrip for having defied doctors' expectations by walking and talking and is inspiring to others for having overcome so much (Easter Seals, n.d.b).

Tori's story is told in this fundraising video to show consumers the successes of Easter Seals programming. Chuck Graham, a U.S. senator featured in the video, says, "I hope that Tori, through her involvement with Easter Seals, is able to have access to all of the therapies and equipment she needs to become the woman that I know she can become" (Easter Seals, n.d.b). The senator, who is also disabled, presents Tori as a once-lost child who has been found through the Easter Seals' assistance in helping her walk and talk. But, unless you donate, she may not be able to become even more of a supercrip and her potential as a productive citizen could be lost forever.

The supercrip does not just uncover her own potential, however, she also acts to unmask the remarkable untapped potential of every non-disabled person. The hopeful reaction of the non-disabled person to a supercrip is intended to trigger a donation because of the self-realization that this disabled person causes in the non-disabled person. This is the realization that the non-disabled person can do so much more — particularly if a disabled person can achieve such remarkable feats.

As a supercrip, the disabled person receives reverence rather than respect and often gains access to the rights that should have been theirs all along. Overcoming disability — while it may come with the consequences of loss of dignity, individuality and/or respect — is beneficial to disabled people in a disablist society.

Of course, the lives of disabled people run the gamut, like everyone, between normal, extraordinary, monotonous, bizarre, dull, eccentric, fantastic, boring and everything in between. Our lives are not constrained to the aspirations of being abled-disabled or to pity and inadequacy. Our motives and ambitions are not dictated by this dichotomy (while we can internalize it and it can heavily influence our sense of self). However, the charity industry constructs disabled lives in this way rather than depicting our lives as the beautiful, diverse, difficult, rewarding lives that they are. While the supercrip and the infantilized, white, pitiful disabled person are problematic and damaging sales pitches, the industry also markets false ideas about resistance and change. They tell us that only you can make the difference that is needed to help make disabled people's lives better.

Segregated Spaces:
Sheltered Workshops and Summer Camps

Two of the programs commonly funded by charity donations are segregated spaces — sheltered workshops and summer camps — that are frequently managed, supervised or policed by non-disabled people. Sheltered workshops employ disabled people and have been described by the National Disability Rights Network, an American advocacy group for disabled people, as "just another institution segregating people with disabilities away because of our unwillingness to accept that our perceived notions about their ability to work may be wrong" (National Disability Rights Network, 2011: 3). These workplaces pay many workers less than minimum wage, are not bound by labour legislation and often act as warehouses for disabled people.

Many disabled workers in sheltered workshops are paid sub-minimum wage, sometimes less than a dollar an hour.[10] For example, one sheltered workshop paid its workers about $30 a month (Gill, 2005). Others shelters pay people "only a few dollars a day" (Clare, 1999: 108), and one American sheltered workshop paid its workers only 8 percent of the minimum wage (Sorrell, 2010), while others make only 10 percent (National Disability Rights Network, 2011). Most workers in sheltered workshops earn half of the minimum wage (National Disability Rights Network, 2011). However, there are even some piecework programs that actually charge disabled people to work for them (Gleeson, 1999). These workplaces are often exempt from labour legislation because the work is understood to be "rehabilitative," a point reflected in the ruling of an Ontario court case involving a Salvation Army workshop:

> [If] the substance of the relationship is one of rehabilitation, then the mischief which the Employment Standards Act has been designed to prevent is not present and a finding that there is no employment

relationship... must be made. (Aszuba and Salvation Army Sheltered Workshop et al., 1983)

This logic has been upheld in at least one provincial appellate court and has withstood the test of time. Where a working relationship is determined to be largely rehabilitative or therapeutic in nature, the jobs that disabled people have are not considered employment. This is the case no matter what those jobs are, how long the workers have been there, how much money the workshop makes or any other factor.

This evaluation is often justified by the assertion that disabled people in sheltered workshops will gain skills through those experiences and move into the "general workforce." However, in the United States, a mere 3.5 percent of people a year actually move out of the sheltered workshop into paid employment (Gill, 2005). This is, in part, because sheltered workshops are businesses. Steven Taylor (2002: n.p.), the director of the Center on Human Policy at Syracuse University, says, "Like any enterprise, workshops need to provide products of high quality to survive and continue to receive contracts. Workshops have a built-in incentive to retain the most productive and dependable clients." Workers who would, even by the workshops' standards, be ready to move into an unsheltered workplace are kept at the workshops in order to increase their profit (Taylor, 2002; Fenton v. Forensic Psychiatric Services Commission, 1991).

I was, however, able to uncover one case of a sheltered workshop worker who was able to make it to the courts regarding a workplace accident. Frank Vanneste had his finger chopped off in a saw at the sheltered workshop where he was employed (*Ottawa Citizen*, 1985). He and a previous manager had both reported that the saw was missing a safety guard. The workshop, which was run by the YM-YWCA, said it didn't have the money to make the saw safe. The board president defended the lack of safety saying that the workers, many of whom were intellectually disabled, had consented to work in unsafe conditions. The court found that Vanneste was not a worker under the law. The court did, however, convict the workshop of one count on the safety issue but suspended the sentence. Ontario's *Occupational Health and Safety Act* continues to consider workers "in a work project or rehabilitation program" not to be workers (section 1 (1)).

Sheltered workshops are more aptly called sweatshops. Sweatshops are workplaces that do not adhere to wage and labour regulations (Liao, 1996). Sheltered workshops do not meet minimum wage standards and workers can be fired for doing things that would not warrant legal dismissal in a regulated workplace — one that isn't a segregated workplace for disabled people (*Izzard v. Cosmopolitan Industries Ltd.*, 2002; Sorrell, 2010).

These workplaces often don't provide full-time work. Indeed, 86 percent of sheltered workshop employees that make sub-minimum wages are under-employed. (National Disability Rights Network, 2011). When there isn't work to be done, some workers are warehoused with little or no programming (one worker was forced to count rocks for no reason but to keep him busy). Yet, when people working in sheltered workshops do move into other employment, their pay and benefits have been found to dramatically increase.

Because these disabled workers aren't considered real workers, they cannot unionize either. In an attempt to unionize Goodwill in Southern California, the National Labor Relations Board found that only the non-disabled employees would be allowed to unionize. This was in spite of the fact that many of the disabled employees had worked there for years and used few of the so-called rehabilitative services (Sorrell, 2010). Charities that run or have run sheltered workshops include Easter Seals, Goodwill, YM-YWCA and the Salvation Army, among others. This is some of the "programming" infrastructure and maintenance that charity dollars fund.

One of the most common examples of charity programming is the summer camp. Many charities run summer camps for disabled children, the most well known of which are perhaps the Muscular Dystrophy Association and the Easter Seals camps. Easter Seals camps have the motto "a place where nobody stares" (Easter Seals Canada, n.d.). While these camps may have a positive or meaningful impact on the lives of disabled children, as any summer camp experience might, these charities construct segregated camp spaces for children, many of whom already attend segregated classrooms or schools. Rather than providing funding or advocacy to ensure that summer camps are accessible, disability charities construct separate camps for kids, providing a stare-less (and stair-less) environment while reinforcing the notion that disabled children are different and legitimizing their separation from other children.

The camps are conducted with continued fundraising in mind. One Muscular Dystrophy Association camp alumni always wondered why MDA donors were "taking pictures of us getting helped" (Erickson, 2010). She also referred to herself as a "cute prop" for the Harley Davidson Motor Company when it attended an MDA camp to let campers sit on motorcycles or in sidecars while taking numerous photos of them for promotional material.

Critics of these camps have seen a small victory with the recent decrease in segregated camps (Goodwin and Staples, 2005). But just because a few segregated camps are closing doesn't mean that disabled kids have more inclusive opportunities. In Ontario, Goodwin and Staples report that "approximately 20% of 200 accredited camp administrators indicates they would like to have their camp name appear on an 'Integrated Camp List'" (2005: 160). This does not necessarily mean that they are fully or partially accessible and even if they are, only about forty camps want to be considered inclusive in a province with a population with over 13 million people.

There are, however, some disabled people who support segregated camps for disabled youth because they allow campers to develop relationships with other disabled people without the influence of non-disabled people. Erickson found going to camp to be a positive experience for this very reason:

> Because it wasn't put on by disabled people for disabled people, there was no attention paid to internalized disablism. We didn't know how to hang out with each other because we had internalized disablism. While there were relationships formed between campers in a way that was empowering it was in spite of the structure of the camp (and larger world). (2011)

Certainly, many disabled people benefit from spaces that are disabled people–only spaces, but these spaces have to be created with the intention of subverting internalization. Like other marginalized groups, disabled people can share experiences based on a common oppression when they are together. It is definitely my experience that I talk about my life very differently when I am with other disabled people. Fiona Campbell (2008: 155) asserts that these spaces "can act as a sanctuary for healing internalized oppression."

There is an important distinction between a space that disabled people create in the spirit of community building and belonging and one that an organization that is led by (primarily) non-disabled people creates for the good of disabled people. As Fiona Campbell (2008: 155) reminds us, "Separation … should not be confused with segregation." Segregation is imposed upon people and the small amount of empowerment that may be gained out of those spaces cannot justify their oppressive nature.

Internalization

Segregated spaces reinforce the idea that disabled people are different, unwanted and unable to exist in the "real world." Disabled people can internalize these ideas, resulting in feelings of inadequacy and insecurity. Further, images of the supercrip and the poor, pitiful, tragic disabled person not only impact public perception of disabled people, they negatively impact disabled people as well. Many disabled people internalize disablism in general and these images in particular. If the only public portrayals of disabled people are those of the infantilized and the pathetic on one hand and the supercrip on the other, this inadequate binary becomes the only framework within which disabled people can interpret themselves. This can lead to disabled people having a skewed sense of themselves.

One way that this can take place is through internalized disablism. This is a form of internalized oppression, which is defined by Penny Rosenwasser as "an involuntary reaction to oppression which originates outside one's group and which results in group members loathing themselves, disliking others in their group, and blaming themselves for the oppression" (in Campbell, 2008: 154). Essentially, internalized oppression is exactly as it sounds: oppression turned inwards.

Internalization works to undermine disabled people's positive identities and impose the identity of a disabled person as depicted by the medical and charity industries. As such, many disabled people feel compelled to aspire to supercripdom or to hide their disabilities. For instance, many blind people work hard to stop doing "blindisms" or habits that are specific to blind people and, therefore, things that remind sighted people that they are blind. Sarah Blake, a blind freelance writer, is the author of the article "Beating Blindisms." In it, she addresses what some blindisms are and how to get people, primarily children, to stop doing them. Blake (2002: 7) writes, "The biggest problem with eye pressing is that it is considered 'socially unacceptable.' It is not something most people do, even though it is probably as 'normal' for a blind person as biting one's nails is for anyone else." Blind people are taught by other blind people to feel shame in doing things that are "normal" for them and to stop doing them in pursuit of normality.

People may also internalize problematic messages from specific charities. For example, the MDA frequently highlights children with forms of muscular dystrophy that are fatal. One person, who is now over thirty years old, with muscular dystrophy says: "[the MDA] gave me a fear of death ... I thought I was going to die at the age of 9 .... Every night I didn't want to go to sleep because I thought I was going to die in my sleep" (Erickson, 2010). According to Harriet Johnson (n.d.), an anti-telethon activist, this is a common experience of many activists with muscular dystrophy. In an effort to maximize fundraising the MDA, discusses muscular dystrophy in very specific and problematic ways that have caused lasting harm to some of the people the organization claims to help.

Internalization can limit disabled people's opportunities. Because of this, we may not have as many skills or as much education as we would have had if we were not disabled. It is important to remember, however, that this is not a result of the presence of disability, it is the result of oppression. Mason (1992) describes this process:

> Internalised oppression is not the cause of our mistreatment; it is the result of our mistreatment. It would not exist without the real external oppression that forms the social climate in which we exist. Once oppression has been internalised, little force is needed to keep us

submissive. We harbour inside ourselves the pain and the memories, the fears and the confusions, the negative self-images and the low expectations, turning them into weapons with which to re-injure ourselves, every day of our lives (in Marks, 1999: 25).

Disabled people's lives can be limited because of internalization. However, this is a very different type of limitation from the ways in which the charity industry portrays disabled people's lives as diminished or limited because of disability.

Charity or Resistance?

Charities also imply that their "helping" is the change that disabled people need and in doing so, they adopt the language of resistance. Like a social justice slogan, a number of cancer charities tell us: "Believe one can make an impact... Strength in numbers" (Enbridge Ride to Conquer Cancer, n.d.), while another says, "The more voices that join together, the louder our rallying cry" (Canadian Cancer Society, 2010). Many organizations tell potential donors they can "make a difference," which almost exclusively entails making a donation (Cystic Fibrosis Foundation, n.d.; Christopher and Dana Reeve Foundation, n.d.).[11] Charities like the Arthritis Society ("Fight It") (Arthritis Society, n.d.), the MDA ("Help fight muscular dystrophy one shamrock at a time") (Muscular Dystrophy Association, 2006: n.p.) and the Canadian Cancer Society ("Join the Fight") (Canadian Cancer Society, 2009–2010: 1) claim that they are fighting disability and disease. Likewise, the American Cancer Society tells us it is "empowering people to fight back" (American Cancer Society, 2010: 12). There are even organizations, like the Foundation Fighting Blindness, the Defeat Diabetes Foundation and the Global Fund to Fight AIDS, Tuberculosis and Malaria that have made their names out of the language of resistance. And, you can "join the movement" to find a cure for multiple sclerosis (Help Me Find A Cure, n.d).

These charities assert that curing the individual is the change we need and that their organization can provide it. At best, charities ignore the social problems that create the very notion of abnormality as well as systemic disablism and other forms of oppression; at worst, they are complicit in covering up these problems as a form of subterfuge with the aim of upholding those systems of oppression.

Akua Benjamin describes this pattern in relation to charities that "assist" Africans:

The images, yes, they portray illness and disease but they do not sufficiently highlight that diseases and illnesses are a result of this history that is embedded of colonization, embedded with a healthy, healthy ongoing dose of racism and the ongoing exploitation and domination by western corporations, aided and abetted by some African leaders to plunder the rich minerals and other resources of Africa, leaving little for people in that part of the world to survive and to survive well. Or, to survive in such a way that they can have the much needed medical supplies for these destitute children in this part of the world. (2005: n.p.)

These charities make appeals to the public for funds while the roots of the problems affecting the people these charities are trying to help — racism, poverty and disablism — are omitted. The quest for change is turned into an individual act of charity rather than a collective act of resistance. The white, North American, disabled child is an object of pity, unable to fulfill her potential within the capitalist system to be a productive economic contributor. The charity model does not question this understanding of people as solely economic producers, nor does it examine or identify the systemic obstacles (employment discrimination, lack of accommodations, segregation, disablism, etc.) that keep people from achieving their "potential."

Samantha King (2001: 117), an extensive researcher of the breast cancer industry, calls charity advertising "a constant flow of images suggesting that the key to solving America's social problems lies in corporate philanthropy, personal generosity, and proper consumption." Consumerism is offered as a solution to the public because, within the charity paradigm, purchasing charity-linked products or making donations will create change. This marketing actively discourages people from taking direct action for actual social change (many, if not most, of these charities list the primary form of volunteering as fundraising) and encourages them to support the status quo, particularly the current economic system.

Stewart Ewen (1976: 81), in his book *Captains of Consciousness: Advertising and the Social Roots of the Consumer,* describes the original aims of advertising as "actively channeling social impulses toward a support of corporation capitalism and its productive and distributive priorities." Moving from this analysis, I argue that mainstream disability charities have become advertising arms for corporations and fulfill an important role in allowing consumer focus to remain in the narrow realm of consumption.

Conclusion

The charity model is an oppressive approach to disability. In theory, it individualizes disability and constructs an idea of disability that is designed to benefit those wanting to feel better about themselves. In practice, it infantilizes disabled people, constructs us as white and reinforces ideological and visual stereotypes of disabled people. The charity industry also works to prop up capitalism through compassionate consumerism and helps to create the image of corporate citizenship when this economic system is intrinsically linked to the oppressive mechanisms that create disability in the first place.

Clearly, disability- and health-linked charities and the charity industry are highly problematic. However, eliminating these organizations without other supports in place would rob some disabled people of the support on which they rely. Conversely, it is very difficult to put the supports people actually need in place while charities continue to create messages about disabled people and our needs that counteract our demands for accessibility, equality and inclusion. The solutions are far from immediate. As we wait and fight for sweeping fundamental change, we must creatively and collectively demand and build successful alternatives to the charity industry.

We need to build strong communities that are inclusive of disabled people that acknowledge disabled people as equals, rather than as objects of pity or inspiration. We need to create accessible and inclusive spaces[12] and work to ensure that people's needs are met publicly with collective, public (rather than private) resources. Further, we need to create interactions between disabled and non-disabled people based on mutual aid and respect.

Ultimately, we will need to make sure that the rubble from this capitalist, colonial empire is cleared from the sidewalks so disabled people can take their proper place in society. In the words of Eli Clare (1999: 12), "Someday after the revolution... disabled people will live ordinary lives, neither heroic nor tragic."

Notes

1. All information is for national organizations and may not reflect local and state chapters (American Cancer Society, 2010; Easter Seals 2009–2010; March of Dimes Foundation. 2010; Muscular Dystrophy Association, 2009A; National Alliance for Research on Schizophrenia and Depression, 2010).
2. All information is for national organizations and may not reflect local and provincial chapters. All data is from the 2009–2010 fiscal year unless otherwise stated (Canadian Cancer Society, 2009–2010; Ontario March of Dimes, 2009–2010; Cystic Fibrosis Canada, 2010; Easter Seals Canada, 2009–2010; Schizophrenia Society of Canada, 2008–2009).
3. Formerly the Canadian Cystic Fibrosis Foundation. Amounts for Cystic Fibrosis Canada for 2009 are from the 2008/2009 annual report.
4. Amounts for 2008–2009.
5. Revenue based on MDA Annual Report, compensation based on CRA numbers.
6. I excluded peer support and conductive education from this calculation because there is no differentiation between peer support for caregivers and for disabled

people. More importantly, conductive education is considered to be an oppressive, flawed practice (Finklestein, 1990). Grants and awards were excluded because they can go to non-disabled people as well.

7. The reference to the amount of calories that an adult with Huntington's disease will require is particularly troubling and harkens back to references of disabled people as "useless eaters" by the Nazis.

8. The term "supercrip" is an alteration of the commonly used (and reclaimed) word "crip." There are problems with this term that many people reclaiming it do not seem to be aware of: that is, it is the name of a gang. CRIPs, which originally stood for Community or Common Resources for Independent People, began as a Black power organization but now is a gang frequently construed as being devoid of politics. Further, "crip" is often used to describe disabled people in general. It is also problematic because it is clearly a physical disability–specific term.

9. Fundraising is so important to Easter Seals that the organization is named after its fundraising initiatives. Easter seals were seals, or stamps, sold at Easter, and in 1967 the organization changed its name from the National Society for Crippled Children to the Easter Seals (Easter Seals, n.d.a).

10. Legislation was introduced in 1996 to prevent sub-minimum wage labour in sheltered workshops in British Columbia but excludes many aspects of sheltered workshop labour. There has been little or no demonstrable change in the lives of disabled workers as a result (Butterworth et al., 2007).

11. "You *can* make a difference every day in your community" (Canadian Cystic Fibrosis Foundation, n.d.) or "You can make a difference" (Christopher and Dana Reeve Foundation, n.d.).

12. All spaces should be inclusive, unless people labelled as disabled do not want to have inclusive spaces. For example, may people in the Deaf community want to have spaces where everyone signs. Also, some disabled people find belonging and freedom in spaces that only have disabled people in them.

Chapter 5

Revolutionizing the Way We See Ourselves

The Rights and Social Models

The three models discussed so far — the eugenic, medical and charity models — are highly problematic. For over a century, disabled people have been organizing outside of these models. In 1880, the National Association of the Deaf (United States) formed, saying, "We have interests peculiar to ourselves which can only be taken care of by ourselves" (Stroman, 2003: 50). The Canadian National Institute for the Blind (CNIB) was started in 1918; it lobbied for services for blind people, and its leadership included people from the blind community.[1] The League of the Physically Handicapped conducted sit-ins and pickets as part of its fight for disabled people's right to work during the Great Depression in the United States (Longmore, 2003). A few years later, the American Federation of the Physically Handicapped (AFPH) was founded. In 1940, the AFPH began to organize for employment and rehabilitation for disabled people (Stroman, 2003).

While there had been small pockets of resistance to the existing primary models of disability, it was not until the 1960s and 1970s that disabled people began crafting their own models in Canada, the United States and Britain. These models initially took divergent paths largely influenced by which side of the ocean people were on. In Canada and the United States, a rights model was first adopted. Meanwhile in the United Kingdom, a social model was developed, which has become the predominant discourse in disability organizing on both continents

The Rights Model

The rights model of disability focuses on human and citizenship rights and ensuring that disabled people have equal access to these rights. Rights, as a concept, developed in the early fifteenth century. However, the word "right" did not exist in the English language until over 400 years later (Young and Quibell, 2000). Today, rights are understood as being a part of one of two broad categories: negative rights and positive rights. According to Young and Quibell

(2000: 749), negative rights are those involving "equality of treatment," while positive rights involve "equality that requires special treatment." That is, positive rights are associated with accessibility and accommodations.

The rights model conceptualizes disabled people as a minority group entitled to all of the same rights and freedoms as non-disabled people. This model focuses on ending discrimination — including linguistic, social and physical barriers — so that disabled people can access their rights. According to Mathew Diller, the rights model is a vitally important infrastructure for addressing the discrimination faced by disabled people:

> The civil rights model posits discrimination and resulting inequality as the central social issues that people with disabilities face. It establishes a framework of relationships in which employers and public institutions have a responsibility to facilitate the social integration of people with disabilities. (2000: 23)

Additonally, this model defines disability as a characteristic, or a perceived characteristic, for which an individual is treated unequally in society.

The rights model focuses on getting disabled people access to society and changing it only as much as is necessary to establish their desired rights; supporters of this movement do not aim to fundamentally restructure society. However, the rights model can be both pragmatic and problematic. Sometimes a rights-model approach is adopted for strategic reasons in order to win gains as part of a broader struggle for social justice. At other times, however, rights models are adopted because the sole aim of those pushing this agenda is to gain more resources and power for a set group of people, which is almost always divisive and politically limiting.

The Disability Rights Movement in the United States

In the 1960s, disabled people in America began to collectively challenge the existing approaches to disability. In particular, the medical model was challenged because it had hegemonic dominance over the definition of disability. Disability organizations drew their inspiration from civil rights and feminist movements.

The history of the disability rights movement in the United States is very rich, and I cannot delve into it in detail here. However, I provide an overview, beginning with Edward Roberts, who attended the University of California at Berkeley in 1963. He sued the school to force them to let him attend. Berkeley didn't want him: Roberts said he was told the university had "tried cripples, and they didn't work" (in Fleischer and Zames, 2001: 38). He and other wheelchair users formed a group called the "Rolling Quads," which fought for physical accessibility for students (Stroman, 2003). In 1972, Roberts went on to head the Center for Independent Living (CIL) in Berkeley. Roberts said:

> Most people never thought of independence as a possibility when they thought of us. But we knew what we wanted, and we set up CIL to provide the vision and resources to get people out [of hospitals, nursing homes and institutions] and into the community. The Berkeley CIL was revolutionary as a model for advocacy-based organizations; no longer would we tolerate being spoken for. (in Fleischer and Zames, 2001: 38)

Independent living activists worked to establish centres for independent living across the United States and throughout the world. In Denver, Colorado, Wade Blank, a former reverend who had been an active supporter of the civil rights movement, began working in a nursing home in 1971. Four years later, he was fired for suggesting that some of the residents be moved into apartments and be cared for there by the facility's orderlies (in Hershey, 1993). After losing his job, Blank helped eighteen residents of the nursing home move out, and together they formed the Atlantis Community (Hershey, 1993). This group was the predecessor for ADAPT (American Disabled for Accessible Public Transit). After winning access to transit, ADAPT changed its name to American Disabled for Attendant Programs. Today, it is one of the most well-known and successful disability rights organizations in the United States. The National Council on Independent Living (U.S.) was founded in 1982. Today, there are hundreds of independent living centres in the United States (Stroman, 2003) and over twenty-five in Canada (Independent Living Canada, n.d.).

The 1970s also saw an escalation of tactics by disability rights activists. Many of these tactics were taken in the United States to ensure the passage of the *Rehabilitation Act,* an important piece of disability rights legislation. Nixon vetoed the proposed law twice, once in 1972 and again in 1973. In 1972, a number of protests were held, including one in New York that included a sit-in on Madison Avenue (Fleischer and Zames, 2001). There was also a protest at the Lincoln Memorial, organized by Disabled in Action and Paralysed Veterans of America, who demanded a debate about disability issues during the 1972 presidential race (Shapiro, 1993). While many disability organizations at the time were divided based on medical diagnostic categories, disabled historian Paul Longmore (2003, 104) claims that the attempts to have the Act passed "prodded [disabled people] to form political alliances across traditionally competitive disability categories. In effect, Nixon provided the nascent disability rights movement with a focus, a unifying target." Ultimately, Nixon signed the *Rehabilitation Act* in 1973.

However, sections 501 to 504 of the *Rehabilitation Act* were passed but not yet enacted. They were sitting on the books, unenforceable until the government chose to enact the necessary regulations. Sections 501 to 503 are related to prohibiting employment discrimination and require affirmative action. Section 504 ensured that disabled people would not be excluded from government-funded programs:

> No otherwise qualified individual with a disability in the United States, as defined in section 7(20), shall, solely by reason of her or his disability, be excluded from the participation in, be denied the benefits of, or be subjected to discrimination under any program or activity receiving Federal financial assistance or under any program or activity conducted by any Executive agency.

This section was crucial to disability rights as, among other things, it would secure access to publicly funded education, including post-secondary schools and transportation.

A group of 120 disabled protestors, many of whom had connections to the Berkeley Center for Independent Living, occupied a U.S. government building in San Francisco in April of 1977 (Fleischer and Zames, 2001; Longmore, 2003). Both the sections of the *Rehabilitation Act* and the regulations for the *Individuals with Disabilities Education Act* were signed on day twenty-three of the sit-in. However, the protesters remained at the sit-in for two days after the signing "in order to be sure they had not been diluted" (Fleischer and Zames, 2001: 55). This landmark victory made it easier for disabled people to fight discrimination and showed the nation that disabled people not only could, but also would, fight back.

The *Rehabilitation Act,* and the later *Americans with Disabilities Act,* would likely never have been passed if not for the disability rights movement. Indeed, many of the gains that disabled people have made over the past thirty years around accessing direct funding for attendant care, moving disabled people back into their communities and access to education (including inclusive classes, accessible transportation, etc.) would likely never have been made if not for the disability rights movement.

The Disability Rights Movement in Canada

The far smaller, but still significant, disability rights movement in Canada has fought for, and won, legal recognition and rights for disabled people. In the 1970s almost all of the provinces had a disability organization and the Coalition of Provincial Organizations of the Handicapped, which is known as the Council of Canadians with Disabilities (CCD) today, was founded in 1976 (Enns, 1999).

Primarily a disability rights lobby, the Council of Canadians with Disabilities, according to its website, "seeks to achieve [its] priorities through law reform, litigation, public education and dialogue with key decision-makers."

One of the major victories of the CCD and other disability rights groups was gaining inclusion in the *Canadian Charter of Rights and Freedoms*. The first draft of the *Charter* did not include disabled people as a group of protected persons. After protests and campaigning, disabled people were added to the *Charter* (Peters, 2003; Vanhala: 2011). As such, governments are prohibited from discriminating against disabled people and disabled people are granted equity rights. Charter inclusion also meant that people who had been disenfranchised because they were confined to institutions (psychiatric institutions, training schools, etc.) were now legally allowed to vote (Stienstra and Wight-Felske, 2003).

The CCD has also waged a longstanding campaign to make public transportation accessible, working to change legislation and actively litigating against VIA Rail and Air Canada (D'Aubin, 2003). It has, in the words of former CCD chairperson Jim Derksen, been "carving out values of inclusion, integration and equality rights" for disabled people in Canada (in D'Aubin, 2003: 88).

Also, members of the CCD were integral in the founding of Disabled Peoples' International (DPI), which got its start in Winnipeg, Manitoba, in 1980. The Rehabilitation International conference in Winnipeg resulted in a walk-out of 200 to 300 disabled delegates who were upset over the lack of representation and leadership from disabled people (Thomas, 1999; Enns: 1999).[2] Henry Enns, a Winnipeg activist who would go on to be the head of DPI, spoke to disabled protestors, saying, "Do I hear you want to form your own international organisation of disabled people?" (Thomas, 1999: 31). These people created DPI, which remains one of the most important disability organizations today.

Problems with Rights-based Approaches

Rights movements are, at their core, about accessing the privileges that a person would otherwise be able to access if they were not a member of an oppressed group. Rights models are reformist; power is to be accessed, not unravelled.

The disability rights movement in the United States (as well as in Canada) began with the intention of gaining access to mainstream society; the movement was a largely (if not exclusively) straight, white, middle-class movement with a strong male leadership. These pioneers were struggling to have the right to access privileged forms of education (university) and to be able to participate in and profit from the capitalist economy. While this movement did focus on ensuring the implementation of positive rights for disabled people, it was (and continues to be) an add-ramps-and-stir approach. Disability rights is not concerned with leaving other disabled people out because they are marginalized beyond just disability.

With oppressive structures intact, rights will only ever take a particular group so far. As Marta Russell (2002: 130) has pointed out, "The market transgresses on nearly every liberal right." She goes on to critique how the *American Disabilities Act* (ADA) has failed reduce the number of unemployed disabled people, calling the system "a fixed game where disabled workers are at the bottom of the competitive labour market and that labour market is, by design, structured to leave millions of workers under-employed and unemployed" (131). Having a right to be free from employment discrimination does nothing to address the capitalist economic system, which requires unemployment to thrive and devalues workers.

However, the rights model can be a pragmatic tool. Obviously, the Canadian and American disability rights movements have won important victories that have changed many disabled people's lives.

The Social Model

In the United Kingdom, many, but not all, disabled activists took a different approach to political organizing. This approach, which was named the social model in 1983 by Mike Oliver (Shakespeare, 2006a), became internationally influential and fundamentally altered disability organizing and how many disabled people saw themselves.

In 1976, in a response to frustrations about existing organizing in England, a group called the Union of the Physically Impaired Against Segregation (UPIAS) wrote the *Fundamental Principles of Disability*, which outlined its political platform. UPIAS defines impairment as "lacking all or part of a limb, or having a defective limb, organism or mechanism of the body" (in Oliver, 1996: 22). This definition has been expanded by most social theory advocates to include mental functioning, mental health, intellectual impairments and sensory impairments (Thomas, 2004a).

For UPIAS, disability is created by a "society which disables physically impaired people." The organization's platform continues: "Disability is something imposed on top of our impairments by the way we are unnecessarily isolated and excluded from full participation in society" (in Oliver, 1996: 33). Under the social model, disability is the oppression that people with impairments face. A common illustration of this point is if your impairment is not having legs, your disability is that you can't get in a building because there is a flight of stairs.

The *Fundamental Principles of Disability* stressed the importance of disabled people's leadership and participation in disability organizations. The document, and UPIAS, also criticized the demand for guaranteed income for disabled people, focusing instead on the importance of disabled people gaining access to paid employment:

> "Benefits" which are not carefully related to the struggle for integrated employment and active social participation will constantly be used to justify our dependence and exclusion from the mainstream of life — the very opposite of what is intended. This is why the … appeal to the state for legislation to implement a comprehensive, national disability incomes scheme is in reality nothing so much as a programme to obtain and maintain in perpetuity the historical dependence of physically impaired people on charity. (in Oliver, 1996: 25)

UPIAS's focus on removing barriers to paid employment is due, in large part, to the Marxist roots of the organization, which put a major emphasis on the economy and labour (Thomas, 1999).

Another tenet of the social model is the idea that disability is not an illness because the model is about the construction of disability and, according to Oliver (1996: 34-35), "there is no causal link" between illness and disability. Oliver (1996: 36) contends that "the problem arises when doctors try to use their knowledge and skills to treat disability rather than illness. Disability as a long-term social state is not treatable medically and is certainly not curable." Under the social model, impairments may be caused by illnesses, and some ill people may be disabled, but disability is a social construct.

The social model was a massively important development as it provided an entirely new way for disabled people to see themselves. It also provided disabled people with a point of commonality. As disability is the oppression that people face, under the social model, there was suddenly a community of disabled people rather than many different communities of people with specific impairments. Disabled people would not only come together when they had a common enemy, like Nixon, they were united together against disability and the social structures that imposed it.

Disabled author Liz Crow described the importance of the social model by illustrating the sense of empowerment it has given to disabled people:

> For years now this social model of disability has enabled me to confront, survive and even surmount countless situations of exclusion and discrimination.… It has played a central role in promoting disabled people's individual self worth, collective identity and political organisation. I don't think it is an exaggeration to say that the social model has saved lives. (1996: 207)

The social model changed how disabled people saw themselves, each other and the world. For this reason, Frances Hasler called it "the big idea" (in Shakespeare, 2006b: 29). Michael Oliver (1996: 30), who claimed "parental rights" for the model, is the academic who fleshed out the UPIAS interpretation of disability. Oliver (2004: 25) said, "The social model was a way of getting us all to think about the things we had in common, and the barriers that we all faced."

Within the grassroots of disability organizing, the social model gained widespread support. However, the established organizations that acted on *behalf* of disabled people, rather than *with* disabled people, were reluctant, even hostile, to the model initially (Oliver, 1996).

Disability organizing took a different turn in England than in the U.S. and Canada because of the differences between the social and rights models. The intention of the social model was not to build or support a rights movement. Vic Finkelstein, one of the original UPIAS members, said, "Civil Rights are about individual people or groups of people — this is a legalistic approach to emancipation. Therefore… the campaign for 'disability rights' does not depend on, nor is it a reflection of, the social model of disability" (2001: 4). Ignoring this contradiction, the disability rights movement in Canada and the United States has adopted the social model definition of impairment and disability and incorporated them into its organizing.

The North American approach is largely a hybrid between the rights and social models. The social model definitions have been adopted by the disability rights movement, which has changed the discourse of the movement to some extent and created the space for much more cross-disability organizing. However, the bulk of North American disability organizing, in my experience, remains civil-rights focused. The disability rights movements in Canada and the United States commonly adopt demands that are geared towards including disabled people in society and stop there. Typically, they do not work for a rebuilding of socio-economic systems, only for them to be rewritten, editing in disabled people as main characters.

Finkelstein, on the other hand, said: "We cannot understand or deal with disability without dealing with the essential nature of society itself. To do this disabled people must find ways of engaging in the class struggle" (5). Very few, if any, disability organizations take this approach to organizing in Canada and the United States.

While the impact of the social model cannot be underestimated, the validity, relevance and representativeness of the model have been questioned. UPIAS was a democratic centralist organization that had a membership consisting of physically disabled people who were primarily living in institutions (Thomas,

1999). This organization and those who championed the social model, most notably Michael Oliver, had a membership of mostly white men.

Critiques of the Social Model

One of the main critiques of this model is its focus on paid labour. For instance, Carol Thomas (1999) asserted that the social model's priority of gaining access to the formal paid workforce excludes many disabled women and their often unpaid labour, including reproductive labour and housework. It also prioritizes certain kinds of help (help for men in the paid workforce) over attendant care to help women perform these gendered forms of labour.

UPIAS's *Fundamental Principles* also publicly attacked another disabled people's organization, Disablement Income Group (DIG), which was fighting for a guaranteed monthly amount of money for disabled people who were "unable to work":

> The alternative to an "incomes" (or more properly, "pensions") approach to the particular poverty in disability is to struggle for changes to the organisation of society so that employment and full social participation are made accessible to all people, including those with physical impairments. (in Oliver, 1996: 24)

This position is highly problematic on pragmatic grounds. While disabled people *can* work, in our disablist, capitalist economy, many disabled people do not work for a variety of reasons, including a lack of accommodation and systemic discrimination. Fighting for social change is essential; however, fighting for long-term change at the expense of people who are immediately trying to access basic needs is not only divisive, it is dangerous. Many disabled people living in the community are in a very vulnerable and precarious position as they are unable to secure adequate food and housing as a result of systemic discrimination and employment discrimination. These are the basic needs that people in DIG were trying to secure for themselves and others. It was problematic for UPIAS members and other proponents of the social model, whose food and shelter were likely not at risk, to publicly organize against these basic demands.

It is possible to be anti-capitalist while advocating for social assistance improvements. Many organizations find the room to fight for long-term social change while fighting to deal with the material emergencies in the communities they work in — first and foremost being the desperate need for money to buy food and pay rent. This struggle can be complementary to the overthrow of capitalism rather than contradictory to it.[3]

Lastly, the *Fundamental Principles* argues that accepting government assistance works to "maintain in perpetuity the historical dependence ... on charity" and compares it to "the begging bowl in modern form" (in Oliver, 1996: 25). This position ignores an important distinction between private (infantalizing and dehumanizing) charity and the distribution of public resources to disabled people, or to anyone in need, within a community. Indeed, economic assistance and redistribution are in line with Marx's principle "From each according to [their] abilities, to each according to [their] needs" (1875: 10). Accepting social assistance does not mean that those disabled people do not work or contribute to their communities; it just means that they find it difficult or impossible to rely on paid labour as a means of survival the way it is structured within our economy. Many disable people choose to subvert the social assistance matrix. Laura Hershey (1993, 159) describes how Wade Blank, a co-founder of ADAPT, encouraged disabled people to "be professional organizers ... Let the government pay your salary, and you go out and organize."

Further, I argue that social modelists' obsession with participation in paid employment (i.e., participation *within* the capitalist system) works to legitimize capitalism rather than undermine it. It also continues to perpetuate the capitalist value that people's worth is connected to their productivity and participation in paid employment. Further, as people are defined as disabled, in part, because of capitalist notions of productivity, it is very problematic to require disabled people to both support and engage in this system.

The Social Model as a Marginalizing Force

Other criticisms of the social model address who and what is left out of the model. The social model was developed by people who are physically disabled and the initial definition made no account for other groups of people who are considered disabled, specifically intellectually disabled people and psychiatrized people. This has resulted, according to Peter Beresford (2004: 209), in a lack of "a strong sense of shared ownership of the social model." The social model was simply expanded to these groups rather than created with them, the same paternalism that the originators of the social model were fighting to eliminate.

Further, the social model does not talk about the body, nor does it talk about impairment beyond defining it separately from disability. The absence of the body in the social model also brought criticism from a number of people who want space to talk about not only their bodies but also their experiences with them. For example, Liz Crow (1996: 209) said, "Bring back impairment! The experience of impairment is not always irrelevant, neutral or positive." Carol Thomas (1999: 25) condemned what she calls the "social modelist tendency to ignore or deny the significance of impairment itself, either in disability theory or in terms of its impact on the daily lives of disabled people." Jenny Morris (1991: 10) wrote that the strong social model works to "deny the personal experience of physical or intellectual restrictions, of illness, of the fear of dying." Because the social model is about disability (as it is defined within the model) the emphasis is solely on the oppressive barriers that disabled people face, and there is a feeling amongst these critics and others that it has erased people's experiences of their bodies.

Indeed, since the early 1990s, there has been an ongoing debate between, primarily, disabled feminists and disabled social modelists.[4] The response of most social model advocates to feminist critiques and the attempt to add the real experience of the body to theoretical and political struggle has, typically, been quite dismissive. Oliver (1996: 35, 42) responded by saying, "Disablement is nothing to do with the body," and by calling on people to "develop a social model of impairment to stand alongside a social model of disability." In other words, the social model is about society, not the body, so not only do people not have to talk about the body, it would be inappropriate to do so. For many, particularly medical modelists, this has been a difficult concept to grasp.

However, this defence strikes many people as being hollow: if disability is imposed upon impaired people, there has to be space to discuss and theorize impairment in non-medical terms. Yet, some have intoned that impairment, or at least people's difficulty with it, is a private or personal issue. Thomas (2004a: 38) argued that there is a "tendency within disability studies to reject what is seen to be public and 'confessional' dabbling in such 'personal or private' matters because this, supposedly, diverts attention away from the 'really important' disabling social barriers 'out there.'" Further, Thomas argues:

> It was this kind of *private/public* split which enabled some male-dominated left-wing political organizations in the 1970s to argue that issues such as *domestic violence*, sexual relationships and women's roles as housewives and mothers were not "rea" political issues because they were about "private" life and belonged to the domestic domain. (1999: 74–75)

These criticisms and increasing pressure from feminists and others to expand the social model appear to consistently have been met with the same dismissive response that Oliver made above.

Many writers have argued that disabled women have been left out. These people frequently also acknowledge the absence of other oppressions in the model. This issue has also been acknowledged by Oliver (2004). However, many feminists commit many of the same erasures that the (mostly) straight, white men that originally developed the social model made by prioritizing one group over others. Carol Thomas (1999, 28), for example, writes that "the experience of disability is always gendered, that disablism is inseparably interwoven with sexism (and racism and homophobia and so on)." In her critique about the absence of women from the social model, she makes only passing reference to disabled women who are also marginalized because of their identities beyond their gender and disabilities, because they are racialized, queer, trans or poor, for example (i.e., the majority of disabled women on the planet). Thomas, like Jenny Morris (1991), Liz Crow (1996) and others, re-creates the same problem that she is critiquing.

The "feminist" critiques of the social model insert the experiences of white women into the model while paying lip-service to other women, functionally perpetuating their oppression. While there has not been substantial theorization about racialization and disability, feminist researchers have worked to replicated this problem through their research. For example, in her qualitative research in *Female Forms: Experiencing and Understanding Disability*, Thomas (1999: 85) fails to adequately include the voices of racialized disabled women, calling this exclusion "a matter of regret."

Further, there has been little attention paid to the critiques of the social model coming from racialized people. These critiques have been limited for a number of reasons, up to and including racism within academia, the publishing industry and the disability rights movement. One open and influential racialized disabled critic of the social model is Parin Dossa. Dossa (2009: 154) recognizes the successes of the social model but argues that they "have been partial, fragmented and discriminatory, as a result both of structural factors and of a hierarchical system that has yet to substantially accommodate the needs and aspirations of racialized women and men." Martin Banton and Gurnam Singh (2004: 113) argue that racialized disabled people can experience a "unique sense of isolation and marginalisation," in part because they may be excluded from both racialized communities and disabled communities; this experience would be compounded for racialized disabled women.

Additionally, racialized disabled people, like others with more than one point of marginality, may face what Stuart (1992: 294) calls "simultaneous oppression." Waqar Ahmad (2000: 113) argued that racialized people may have a number of experiences of oppression in common with white people, but "the intensity and persistence of disadvantage that minority ethnic users face can be understood only with reference to their racialized worlds." The social model fails to take any of these perspectives into account and fails to recognize any forms of intersecting oppressions.

O.W. Stuart (1992) also offers insights into the key ways that disablism and racism is compounded for racialized disabled people. Stuart (1992: 298) argues that racialized disabled people do not typically experience social fraternity and "are not fully incorporated into this society" because of racism.

This includes (largely white) disability organizing. At the same time, many Black disabled people also experience social exclusion within their racial and/or ethnic communities on the grounds of disability, leaving them very isolated. Further, disabilities are given different meanings when read on Black bodies as compared white bodies. Stuart (1992: 301) says that Black disabled people are "assumed to 'suffer' from alien cultural practices; which are assumed to account for their incidence of impairment." The racist and disablist lens that racialized people are viewed through by mainstream society may attribute their disabilities to racially stereotyped activities such as violence, poor nutrition and lack of hygiene. Black disabled people also experience discrimination when resources are allocated. While Stuart focuses solely on Black disabled people, much of this analysis can be extended to other racialized disabled people in Canada and the United States, as his arguments broadly address racism and racialization, as opposed to a specific experience limited to Black disabled people. None of these experiences, however, are incorporated in the social model.

The Social Relational Model

While failing to incorporate criticism coming from racialized people, the social relational model of disability builds on the social model by incorporating a number of the feminist critiques. One of the originators of the social relational model, Carol Thomas (2004a: 35) asserts that "'disability,' 'impairment' and 'being normal' come into being through their social performance, and on the power that these categories have in constructing subjectivities in identities of self and other." Proponents of this model argue that the focus on the material world in the social model does not appropriately address the full experience of being disabled and its psycho-social consequences. Donna Reeve (2004: 89) argued that a relational model acknowledges the "unconscious and insidious effects on the psycho-emotional well-being of disabled people and because it has a direct impact in restricting who someone can 'be.'" This approach has room to acknowledge the importance and impact of internalized oppression as well as inter-personal and cultural barriers. People are restricted because they experience barriers, because they are oppressed and because they restrict themselves in anticipation of, or belief in, that oppression. These components make the social relational model more inclusive to psychiatrized people and intellectually disabled people, who don't frequently experience physical barriers like stairs or small fonts to be disabling. All disabled people are susceptible to oppression from social interactions.

The social relational model not only acknowledges that some people have difficulty with their impairments, but also welcomes the conversation about people's experiences of their impairments. Jenny Morris (2001: 9) argued that "the majority of physically disabled people feel unwell most of the time," and not talking about impairment erases disabled people's experiences. Morris favours a model that allows people to live and talk about the "actual experiences of our bodies."

Added into the social relational model is the idea of restricted activity or impairment effects. Thomas (1999: 38) calls for the acknowledgment that "*some* restrictions of activity are caused by limited physical, sensory or intellectual functioning." She argues that impairment may actually involve its own limitations to activity, beyond the restrictions imposed by disablism. There are three main components within the social relational model as Thomas proposes it: impairment ("socially marked as unacceptable bodily deviation") (2004a: 41), impairment effects (limitations or restricted activity as a result of impairment) and disability (barriers that are "wholly social in origin"), which includes internalized oppression (2004b: 581). For example, if someone uses a wheelchair because they have a spinal chord injury, this model identifies the spinal chord injury as impairment, their inability to walk as an impairment effect and discrimination and the fact that the person may not try certain things because of fear of discrimination and their inability to build relationships as a result of discrimination, stereotypes and physical barriers as disability.

Tom Shakespeare (2006b: 41) calls the difficulty that disabled people face because of their impairments an "intrinsic limitation." Shakespeare believes this makes disabled people different from other oppressed groups and makes disablism different than other oppressions:

> The oppression which disabled people face is different from, and in many ways more complex than, sexism, racism and homophobia. Women and men may be physiologically and psychologically different, but it is no longer possible to argue that women are made less capable by their biology. (41)

This position upholds the notion that there is a biological basis to the oppression of disabled people. Morris argues that some disabled people may find it "inherently distressing" to have an impairment, while this is not the case for other groups. However, it is problematic to make assumptions about natural or biological difference, and it is dangerous to use it to explain part or all of a group's oppression. The idea of inherent hardship is not actually about disabled people; it is about what is constructed as normal and what is constructed as different because it is too far away from the norm.

While Shakespeare argues that it is impossible to argue that women are biologically inferior to men, the reality is that people continue to make this argument. Former Harvard President and member of U.S. President Obama's

Economic Council, Lawrence Summers (2005: 5), says "there are issues of intrinsic aptitude" that explain why women are less represented in the top levels of sciences. Summers does argue that women have an inherent hardship due to their substandard biology.

Conversely, the *Western Report* (1995: 35) asserted that "women, as an example, can reasonably be defined as ordinary citizens. But criminals, homosexuals and the mentally crippled are by nature extraordinary, not ordinary." So, to this author, there would be some form of inherent difference for homosexuals and criminals as well as certain disabled people. Who might be put on the list of extraordinary people — those of us who are abnormal or not ordinary — tells us something about the people making this list rather than the people on it. Any marginalized group could be, and has been, swapped out for another on this list of people considered to be extraordinary.

Thomas (2004a: 42) defines restricted activity as being "judged against socially defined age norms." Thomas doesn't define what age norms are; presumably, any activity that one is below average at performing for their age group (likely, one standard deviation or more) would constitute a restricted activity. At the core of the conceptualization of the social relational model is the idea of "restricted activity" versus "normal activity." So, relationalists give positive value to the norm as they define restricted activity and, hence, disability in negative terms.

The Social Model and Impairment/Disability: A False Dichotomy

The social relational model also continues to perpetuate what, to me, is the social model's biggest flaw: the impairment/disability binary. UPIAS and Oliver, among others, present a framework that puts forward impairment as the biological reality — that is, the things that are *wrong* with us. This model, while purporting to demand extensive social change, fails to question impairment itself and accepts the medical model as it is applied to impairment (Shakespeare, 2006b).

The social model fails to attribute any kind of social meaning on impairment itself. Advocates of this theory argue we should focus on the social construction of disability and combat the factors that allow the creation of disability, instead of addressing impairment. However, focusing on the model's formalization of disability and maintaining the distinction between disability and impairment will fail in defeating the factors that create disability.

Impairments, as defined by UPIAS, are impairments because of the context in which they are understood, not because they are biological certainties. For example, for many years homosexuality was considered a mental illness.

In fact, it was originally considered psychopathy (Marcus, 1992) and was later listed specifically as its own mental illness (Silverstein, 2008). Under the impairment/disability dichotomy, homosexuality is the impairment and homophobia is the disability. However, homosexuality is only an impairment in as much as we ascribe negative meaning to certain people's attractions. This may seem like a cop-out example, but the point is that homosexuality really was an impairment at one point, and it is not generally understood to be an impairment now in Canadian and American society because our social values and power structures have changed.

Likewise, in a world with a built environment that did not include stairs, a wheelchair user would not be disabled under the social model, but that person would also not be viewed as impaired under the model's definition, at least not in the same way. The social model defines impairment as having "a defective limb" (UPIAS in Oliver, 1996: 22), but in a world without stairs a wheelchair user may not be understood as having a "defective limb" or as having an impairment in the same way as it is understood in a staired world.

As disability has shifted through history, so too has impairment in its functional sense. While the social model is an improvement over the previous thoughts on disability that labelled us as entirely defective, it continues to label us as partially defective.

There have been calls for a rejoining of impairment and disability. Tom Shakespeare and Nicholas Watson (2001) have compared the impairment/ disability dichotomy to the sex/gender dichotomy that was used by second-wave (and some third-wave) feminists. However, feminists like Judith Butler (1999) have criticized this approach, arguing that sex, too, is a social construct. Increasing attention has been paid to disability theory by postmodernists who question both the impairment/disability dichotomy and the belief that there is a biological certainty to the body. Shakespeare and Watson (2001: 16) have said that "the words we use and the discourses we deploy to represent impairment are socially and culturally determined. There is no pure or natural body, existing outside of discourse."

Conclusion

The impairment/disability dichotomy, like the sex/gender dichotomy was very useful at one time, but it is no longer appropriate. The social theory was important to create disability movements and fight for change. My life is better for it, and I owe the utmost respect to the people who developed the social model. But, it is our second wave. The social model has begun to get to the base of issues and move past the immediacy of first-wave goals; however, it continues to replicate a number of oppressions and maintain problematic and false binaries.

The social model was a groundbreaking conceptualization of disability that broke from all of the models before it. Its central idea was that disability and impairment were separate and that understanding disability as a social phenomenon helped create space for disabled people to unify and organize in new ways.

Both the social model and the disability rights model have led to a plethora of positive changes in disabled people's lives. Without them, many disabled people would not have been able to access education, housing, transportation, the electoral system or communities. However, these models are rooted in problematic and outdated ideologies. Without them, we would not be where we are today, but it is time to move beyond the limiting rights and social models and formulate new, radical ways of understanding disability.

Notes

1. While the CNIB was founded by two rich, sighted people, it had blind members on the board. According to Boyce et al. (2001: 15), "The CNIB was the first national Canadian organization led by persons with disabilities." However, as its founders were not disabled, it is unclear how much of the leadership was actually coming from blind people. Further, this is not by any means an endorsement of the CNIB as it is now.
2. Thomas says 200; Enns says 300.
3. For example, see the work of the Ontario Coalition Against Poverty, <www.ocap. ca>.
4. This began, to my knowledge, with Jenny Morris's 1991 book *Pride Against Prejudice: Transforming Attitudes to Disability*. I caution here against ascribing these arguments to a feminism of disability model, as there are many approaches to feminism. Just because a number of prominent feminists have laid similar critiques to the social model does not mean that a feminist model of disability has emerged. While these critiques fall within a feminist framework, so too does the radical model, described in the next chapter.

Chapter 6

Looking Back but Moving Forward

The Radical Disability Model

None of the models discussed so far have adequately addressed both disablism and disabled minds and bodies; rather, they focus either on the oppression we experience (social model) or on what the models define as our flawed bodies and/or minds (eugenic, medical and charity models). This final chapter discusses the radical model of disability, my proposal for bringing disability politics into a new wave. This framework, while based on the work of a number of disabled activists and scholars (notably Clare, 1999; Davis, 1995, 2002; Moore, 2002; Erickson, 2007; Epstein, 2009) as well as feminist, anti-racist, anti-capitalist and postmodern theory, is relatively new. Developed in organizing meetings and coffee shops in Toronto, it is my proposal for how we should move disabled people's movements forward and how anyone concerned with social justice should conceptualize disability.[1] It is also a call to action, for disabled people and non-disabled people alike, to organize inclusively for social justice and radical access.

The radical model defines disability as a social construction used as an oppressive tool to penalize and stigmatize those of us who deviate from the (arbitrary) norm. Disabled people are not problems; we are diverse and offer important understandings of the world that should be celebrated rather than marginalized.

There are four key concepts in the radical model. Firstly, disability is not separate from other forms of oppression; rather, it is interlocked with and overlaps them. Secondly, what is considered normal is arbitrary and requires deconstruction. Up until this point, all of the models of disability have failed to challenge the supremacy of the norm. Margrit Shildrick and Janet Price (1998: 236) have written, "A more radical politics of disability, then, would disrupt the norms of dis/abled identity... by exposing the failure of those norms to ever fully and finally contain a definitive standard." Thirdly, the disability label is used to marginalize specific types of people in order to obtain and maintain power; the classification of disabled is a political determination, not a biological one. Disability is not about whether or not something is "wrong" with someone; it is about the classification of disability, which allows certain people to be marginalized and other people to both benefit from that marginalization and justify it, because the rest of us are inferior. Lastly, accessibility cannot be addressed universally; rather it must be approached holistically.

While the medical model presents disability as falling somewhere on a spectrum between full health and the absence of it, the radical model posits that, to borrow Foucault's (1969) concept, disability falls somewhere in a constellation. Like the constellations in the sky, disability is in constant flux and appears different depending on the positioning of the onlooker.

This model rejects the social model's distinction between impairment and disability. To review: "impairment" is defined by the social model as functional limitations and "disability" as the oppression "imposed on top of our impairments" (UPIAS in Oliver 1996: 33). The radical model of disability rejects the notion that impairment is a biological reality. The radical model also posits that impairment and disability can necessarily be distinguished from each other. This model is not the social model of impairment — while the model has a strong focus on the social construction of impairment it rejects the dichotomies created by the social model.

In some times, places or cultures, having visions is viewed as wholly negative, requiring the individual to undergo medical intervention, confinement, medication and/or forced electric shocks to the head. In other times, places or cultures, it is seen as a gift. Similarly, deafness is understood to be a disability by the medical model but for some people this has been far from the case. For instance, in Martha's Vineyard around the turn of the last century "everyone… spoke sign language," according to Gale Huntington, who lived there at the time. The townspeople "didn't think anything about [Deaf people], they were just like everyone else" (in Groce 1985: 2). Deafness was perceived very differently and not as a disability in the way that it is in a community where most hearing people are unable to communicate with Deaf people. What is considered a disability depends on the context.

Intersectionality

A foundational component of the radical model is the idea of intersectionality: addressing multiple oppressions together and in conjunction with each other. The word "radical" is derived from the Latin, meaning "having roots." A conceptualization of disability that did not include, at its base, the acknowledgment of and engagement with the interlocutory nature of oppressions could not be a radical model.

Within disability theory, intersectionality is often ignored. For instance, disability studies have been called "white disability studies" (Bell 2010: 374), and the exclusion of women in that discipline has already been documented. Eli

Clare writes further on the lack of intersectionality in radical disability circles:

> Unfortunately, not many disability or nondisabled progressive groups engage in multi-issue thinking and organizing that deeply embeds disability politics into an agenda that includes race, class, gender, and sexuality. At an ADAPT demo recently, I saw a flyer that read "You think prison is bad, try a nursing home." In one simple slogan, disability activists advanced a hierarchy of institutions and oppressions, defined disability as their sole focus, and revealed profound ignorance about the ways being locked up in prisons cause bone-crushing damage, particularly in communities of color. This slogan and the disability politics behind it leave little chance for making connections and addressing the daily complexities of folks who know the grief and outrage of both prisons and nursing homes. (2009: 12)

Disability politics often re-establish whiteness, maleness, straightness and richness as the centre when challenging the marginality of disability. Similarly, when disability studies writers discuss other oppressions, they often do so as distinct phenomena in which different marginalities are compared (Vernon, 1996b; Bell, 2010).

When oppressions are discussed in an intersectional road, it is commonly treated like a country road: two, and only two, separate paths meet at a well-signed, easy-to-understand location. Typically, authors talk about disability and women (see Thomas, 1999; 2004a; 2004b; Rohrer, 2005; Wendell, 1989, 1996; Crow, 1996; Morris, 1991; Fine and Asch, 1988; Gill et al., 1994; Hall 2002; Garland-Thomson, 1994), disability and class (see Stewart and Russell, 2001; Preece, 1996), disability and race (see Bell, 2010; Stubblefield, 2009; Stuart, 1994) and disability and queerness (see McRuer 2002, 2003a, 2003b; Clare, 2001; Sandahl, 2003). None of these lists is complete, and there are, of course, some important exceptions to the common practice of over-simplifying intersectionality (Vernon, 1996a, 1999; Clare, 1999; Garland-Thompson, 2002, 2005; Emmett, 2006; Petersen, 2006; Sherry, 2007; Clare, 2009; Dossa, 2009; Mingus, 2011).[2]

Intersectionality is a multi-lane highway with numerous roads meeting, crossing and merging in chaotic and complicated ways. There are all different kinds of roads involved: paved and gravel roads, roads with shoulders and those without and roads with low speed limits, high speed limits and even no speed limits. There is no map. The most important feature of these intersections, though, is that they look very different depending on your location.

With respect to multiply oppressed people, Chris Bell (2010: 378) points out that their ethnicity and race are erased, "letting them be run over, forgotten."

This is the case for many people with more than one marginality, yet disabled organizers and academics in the field of disability studies negate our complex identities. When disabled people are "run over" because our identities are omitted, it is no accident. These erasures occur for a number of reasons: prejudice, ignorance and/or an attempt to distance a group from others in order to better lay claim to privilege.

Being real about intersectionality means working to keep people from being "run over," as Bell puts it. One way people get run over or left out occurs when some members of the disabled community talk about "disability culture." "Culture" can be used in lots of ways and mean lots of different things. It is important, however for everyone to recognize that they are a part of a culture. Sometimes white people don't acknowledge that they are a part of a culture because it is so pervasive and dominant that it can be hard for some people to recognize. When disabled people talk about disability culture it is important that they not erase the many cultures that many disabled people are a part of.

Out from Under Disability

It is highly problematic for disabled people to simply build a rights movement to access privilege; yet this has largely been the case in Canada and the United States. Equally problematic are groups of people who are classified as disabled working to take themselves out from under the disability umbrella in order to build a rights movement to access privilege. Many different groups that fall or have fallen under the disability umbrella have worked to separate themselves from the category of disability to their advantage and to the disadvantage of those they leave behind.

Since in the 1970s, Deaf people have fought to get out from under the disabled label (Baynton, 2002). According to *A Journey into the Deaf-World* by Lane, Hoffmeister and Bahan (1996: 232), "To be Deaf is not a disability in Deaf culture, and most members of the Deaf-World see no disability in their way of being." Or, as M.J. Bienvenu has put it "We are proud of our language, culture and heritage. Disabled we are not!" (in Lane, 1995: 83). This statement not only works to separate Deaf people from the disabled identity, but it also implies that there is no pride in a disabled identity.

Psychiatric survivor activists have been working to unaffiliate with the disabled community. This movement has asserted that there is nothing wrong with psychiatrized people and, therefore, they are not disabled. Beresford, Gifford and Harrison argue in *Speaking Our Minds* that this is because they understand their disability label as being imposed from above by medical professionals:

Many psychiatric system survivors are unwilling to see themselves

> as disabled. They associate disability with the medicalization of their distress and experience. They reject the biological and genetic explanations of their distress imposed by medical experts. They may not see themselves as emotionally or mentally distressed either, but instead celebrate their difference and their particular perceptions. (1996: 209)

Because many psychiatric survivors and mad pride organizers have disablist assumptions about disability and disabled people, they frequently argue that they are not a part of the disabled community. Additionally, a number of the campaigns against forced drugging and ECT invoke disablist arguments to advance their case (Withers, 2010). Psychiatric survivors have problematized the medical model as it applies only to them, identifying it as abusive and a tool for social control in relation to the psychiatric aspects of medicine (Burstow and Weitz, 1988; Burstow, 2006), not to the other aspects of the medical model or the model as a whole.

The trans (transgender, transsexual, genderqueer et al.) community is a group of people that has been psychiatrized but, on an organizational level, does not work with psychiatric survivors to achieve non-disabled status. Rather than being protected on the grounds of gender or sex, trans people have human rights protections in New York (and possibly other states) because "GID [gender identity disorder] is a disability" under state law (*Doe v. Bell*, 2003: n.p.). Trans people are pathologized under the category of gender identity disorder (GID); our identities are funnelled through medical "treatments." This process is undermining, arduous and can be abusive (particularly with respect to children). Some trans activists are fighting for the removal of GID from the DSM so transsexuality would no longer be a disability. Dr. Kelly Winters (in GID Reform Advocates, 2005) argues that the diagnosis "stigmatizes [trans people] unconditionally as mentally deficient." She continues: "Difference is not a disease, nonconformity is not a pathology, and uniqueness is not an illness." (This is the same argument that disabled people make about disability).

Interestingly, however, there is no consensus on this point. The reason for dissent is the realization that many trans people are poor and cannot afford sex reassignment surgeries (and, to a lesser extent, hormones), which they would not have access to without the pathologization of the trans identity.

As a disabled trans person, I believe the trans community should adopt a radical disability perspective and view (other) disabled people as allies. I think the trans community should fight for medical care without pathologization and use this discussion as a way of challenging the medical system and the existing power structures that the medical system moulds its perspectives to. Nevertheless, there are many trans people fighting to take us (or those of us who aren't otherwise disabled) out from under the disability umbrella.

Trans and other psychiatrized people, along with Deaf people, have set out to counter the stigma attached to disability and to build a rights movement by arguing that there is nothing wrong with them; ergo, they are not disabled. Trans people argue that there is nothing wrong with them, they experience their bodies and genders in ways that do not align with so-called biological standards; psychiatric survivors argue that there is nothing wrong with them because they experience or are perceived to experience the world differently; Deaf people argue that there is nothing wrong with them because they are a linguistic minority. These arguments do not contradict the radical disability model whatsoever. However, with Deaf, trans and psychiatrized people saying that they are not disabled because there is nothing wrong with them, they work to reinforce the idea that there is something wrong with those disabled people they are trying to distance themselves from.

While Deaf, trans and psychiatrized people are working toward becoming non-disabled, other groups have been far more successful. As already discussed, women were classified as unfit or disabled during the eugenic era. Feminists fought for women's rights and in doing so worked to construct themselves as nondisabled, reinforcing the oppression of those they left behind. Many feminists have perpetuated the construction of women as strong, non-disabled people, saying things like, "Female physical frailty is not a reality but a myth with an agenda" (Dowling, 2000: 213).

Racialized people have also worked to distance themselves from disability. Erevelles, Kanga and Middleton (2006: 78–79) have written about some critical race thinkers who "have actively sought to distance race from any associations with disability because they have recognized that this association has been used to justify the brutality of slavery, colonialism, neocolonialism and the continued exploitation of people of color." The disability label has been used in horrifyingly violent, even genocidal, ways against racialized people. However, the problem is not disabled people; rather, it is the disability label, and choosing not to talk about it does nothing to disassemble the power structures that allow it to exist. Some anti-racists have also argued that it is "demeaning to racial groups" to connect disability struggles to anti-racist struggles (Erevelles, Kanga and Middleton, 2006: 79).[3] Of course, this perspective is demeaning to disabled people and only works to strengthen the idea that we are separate and should remain separate.

The mainstream gay rights movement was also successful in being declassified as disabled. While the medical industry had pathologized homosexuality and homosexuals out of hatred, ignorance and desire for social control, homosexuals looked to this same profession, and specifically to psychiatrists, to de-pathologize and socially legitimize them. In the 1960s, organized gays and lesbians took an active role in fighting for change. One of the key aims of the struggle was to establish homosexuality as a minority group rather than a disability. The mainstream gay rights movement argued that the categorization of disability needed to become one of the key battlegrounds in the rights movement (Kameny, 2009).

The mainstream gay rights movement built itself through its separation away from other marginalities and its separation from the disability umbrella.[4] In establishing homosexuals as non-disabled, the movement actively organized against being defined as disabled, as well as being against those who defined homosexuals as disabled: the American Psychiatric Association (APA). The APA was the gatekeeper of all psychiatric diagnoses and had the power to un-psychiatrize homosexuality. This criticism was not of pathologization or the oppressive nature of the classification of disability in general, simply that those in power had erred in classifying *them* as disabled. This strategy actually worked to maintain disablist oppression and the status quo while negotiating privileged homosexuals' co-optation.

In 1973, the mainstream gay rights movement was successful in getting homosexuality de-listed as a psychiatric disability. Gay psychiatrist Charles Silverstein (2008: 272) called it "the most important achievement of the Gay Liberation Movement." Out of this, a new "minority rights" movement was born. Homosexuals would no longer be forcibly confined, electro-shocked, drugged, lobotomized and subjected to other horrors simply for being homosexual. Undoubtedly, this is an incredibly important victory in the history of gay rights and one I personally benefit from. However, it is important to examine it critically. It was a victory for many homosexuals at the time, but a lot of homosexuals were left behind.

To be gay or lesbian is no longer to be pathological, as white, middle- and upper-class homosexuals and bisexuals (especially gay men) are considered to be productive and useful in contemporary society (particularly the "straight acting" gays or "strays"). The mainstream movement has rallied around assimilationist issues like gay marriage, gays in the military (in the United States) and adoption that work to uphold capitalist values and social norms. This is done instead of, and at times at the expense of, organizing in defence of (or even actively marginalizing) "deviant" queer lifestyles like polyamoury, sex work, transsexuality, transgenderism and gender queerness that challenge those values and norms. Many of these ways of living remain psychiatrized and are still considered disabilities. That said, there remains strong opposition on the political right to the integration of "strays" into mainstream society.

The mainstream gay rights movement sold out its disabled members (not to mention its racialized and poor, trans, intersexed, two-spirited and, oftentimes, women members).[5] Racialized communities and women also sold out many members of their communities in order to access privilege by winning the status of non-disabled.

Griffin Epstein (2009: 33) says that there is a "national mandate for the formerly marginalized to pick up the mantle of the oppressor in exchange for the rights and privileges of citizenship." With respect to disability, all of these groups (women, racialized people, homosexuals, trans and other psychiatrized people and Deaf people) have taken up that mantle in order to win reclassification as non-disabled. Those groups that have won a level of marginality that does not include being called disabled largely continue to uphold disablism and maintain separation from disabled people. Indeed, Davina Cooper (2009: 233) argues: "When one minority group tries to seek equality by breaking away from the stigma produced by association with another group, the claim of equality can further naturalize the other minority group's alienation." This act of separation often serves to reinforce the justification for the oppression of those left behind.

Of course, there are many disabled people who are also members of these groups that have been left behind in these definitional shifts. Beyond continuing to oppress other members of these marginalized groups, there are other reasons that make the struggle to reconstruct these groups as non-disabled problematic. Of course, it is always problematic and disappointing (yet, almost predictable) for marginalized groups to participate in the oppression of other marginalized groups. Rather than working in coalitions to challenge the systems that permit the characterization of undesirable people as disabled, these groups have created space for their communities to be at perpetual risk of being reclassified as disabled on other grounds as the needs of those in power shift.

Threats of being placed back under the disability umbrella are real for racialized communities, women and homosexuals. Academics like Rushton and Jensen have devoted their careers to proving the intellectual inferiority of, particularly, Black people to build the case that they are disabled. The prospect of the re-pathologization of women has recently become an issue because of prenatal sex selection. Also, the discovery of a "gay gene," which is actively being sought, could lead to the re-pathologization of homosexuality. These are just some of the ways that these communities could be reclassified as disabled.

Because components of these movements have worked to reinforce the idea that disability (and by extension disabled people) is bad and undesirable, they will be left with few political options if they face re-pathologization. Further, these groups all share overlapping populations, so, racialized queer women are especially at risk of being put back into the disability box.

Adopting a radical model of disability, rather than trying to break out of the disability category, would problematize the entire disability labelling process, not just a few communities' membership within it. Successfully eliminating the systems that permit the creation of the category of disability would leave every member of all of these marginalized groups better off.

Of course, the reinforcing of oppression in order to get out from under the disability label is only one way that marginalized groups work to uphold the oppression of others. There are countless examples of when and how oppressed groups (including disabled people) have targeted or tried to oppress each other for rights and resources. This is because, according to Martin Banton and Gurnam Singh (2004: 113), "oppressed groups often succumb to" oppressive ideologies. One of the consequences of this is that the group "may seek to identify a position within the strata that is superior to as many other groups as possible." When this happens, according to Banton and Sing, oppressed communities can act to "reinforc[e] the structures of oppression."

Disabled people are not immune to this phenomenon. Disability organizations in Canada and the United States have frequently "picked up the mantle of oppression" and allowed themselves to be co-opted, rather than build their struggles outward. There are numerous examples of those groups still well under the disability umbrella trying to distance themselves from others to gain privilege. Some physically disabled people were against advocating for the inclusion of people who were psychiatrized or intellectually disabled in the *Charter of Rights and Freedoms* because it could lower their chances for inclusion (Vanhala, 2011). There has also been a great deal of criticism of the disability rights movement for being dominated by physically disabled people.

There is also a Facebook group called "Being physically disabled does not automatically make us stupid." It tells people to "join this group and together we can make people change their attitudes towards us." The attitudes that are being changed, though, are the disablist attitudes about others — and these attitudes are being reinforced. I have also seen physically disabled people who are the brunt of disablism say that they are smart or that they have a university degree to assert their worth.

On the other hand, I know physically disabled people who have been the subjects of pity from intellectually disabled people who operate on the assumption that they have it so much worse. Many intellectually disabled people identify as "people who have been labelled" (People First of Canada, 2006). The choice to refer to themselves as "people who have been labelled" without using the word "disabled" reinforces the idea that there is something negative about being disabled, while addressing the root of the problem, or the fact that the label exists, is out of their control. I think it is important to respect the way that people choose to identify. At the same time, I am critical of this choice as it seems to me to be rooted in disablism.

This competitive oppression-building is also performed by disability organizations towards those groups that have moved outside of the category of disability. Just one example is how, in Canada and the United States, disabled organizations have fought for "accessible" public transit; but once ramps, lifts and automatic announcement systems have been put in place, they stop fighting. These organizations don't fight for free or affordable transit or an end to discrimination on public transit, to name but a few causes.[6] Movements for change cannot continue to replicate the models of co-optation and oppression.

Disability is not actually about those of us who are disabled; it is about those with the power to call us disabled. Indeed, marginality is controlled by those who are not marginalized, which makes it very important to work collectively as oppressed groups to target that power. Further, one cannot choose to only fight disablism, as most disabled people experience more than one form of marginalization and, therefore, more than one form of oppression.

This is why poverty, sexism, heterosexism/homophobia, transphobia, racism and ageism must be fought in tandem. Internationally, most disabled people are racialized (New Internationalist, 2005; Parens et al., 2009). In Canada, rates of disability are disproportionately high among First Nations people, racialized people and non-European recent immigrants (Raphael, 2007). Also, most disabled people are women — they are more likely than men to report chronic conditions and disabilities (Federal, Provincial and Territorial Advisory Committee on Population Health, 1999; Raphael, 2007). Disabled people are far more likely to be poor than non-disabled people (Rosano et al., 2008; Raphael, 2007; OECD, 2010). Many of us are queer and/or trans, and most of us are seniors. Our multiple identities means that if we focused solely on disablism, much like aspects of the disability rights movement has done, then we are working to exclude the majority of disabled people from our struggle — people who would not be able to access the privileges that they would be able to access if they were not disabled.

It is important not only to acknowledge the diversity within disabled communities, but also to act in solidarity with other movements. The disability rights and social models have largely failed to fight other oppressions and to work in solidarity with other marginalized groups and anti-oppression movements for change. Rather than fighting for our piece of the pie while working to enforce existing oppression on others, we need to bake a new pie. We have to build new models. To quote longtime activist Beric German (2009), "It cannot just be pie in the sky, it has to be pie that you can eat."

Normal, Biological and Political Constructions

Disability, which includes impairment, is a social construct. In U.S. and Canadian societies, our disabilities are defined by those in power to their own advantage. Who and what counts as disabled shifts depending on what power dictates, oftentimes with broad, sweeping definitions in order to marginalize people. In this society, power and capitalism are intrinsically related. Those in power enable capitalism to function, and capitalism enables those in power to keep their power and obtain more of it. According to Sam Gindin (2002: n.p.), "Some people control the potential of others, control how that potential develops over time, privately appropriate the surplus created in social production, and apply that surplus to restructure work, communities, and future opportunities." It is these elites that also control the definition of what is normal and, therefore, what is disabled, in order to maintain and expand influence and control to their benefit. The definition of disability shifts as the needs of those in power shift: as economic and social needs change, so too does the classification of who is disabled. People who are disabled are labelled so because people with power say we are disabled.

Since the advent of eugenics, one of the primary reasons we have been, and continue to be, categorized as disabled is because we are considered to be unproductive or under-productive in the capitalist system. In practice, capitalism is a system that is upheld by a number of myths. One of them is that white people are superior to racialized people. Another is that men are superior to women (also that there are only women and men as far as gender identities go and that those identities are fixed). Capitalism is not necessarily patriarchal and racist; however, the current form of capitalism that operates globally is inherently patriarchal and racist. All forms of capitalism, however, are innately oppressive and work to benefit the few at the expense of the many. Also, there is a myth that some people have power and wealth because they work hard and others are lazy and that there is one ideal that people must strive to achieve.

In order to maintain our belief in the capitalist myths, they need to be socially imposed. Those of us who violate the goal of striving for the ideal (by choice or by our existence, as is the case with many disabled people) or who challenge our roles within the socio-economic system face consequences for our deviance. Sometimes these consequences are legal, such as forced confinement and "treatment" of many psychiatrized people, but more often they are economic and social. We are made into examples; we are denied the resources, joys, comforts, jobs and pleasures that "normal" people have access to. We are then punished for our low productivity by way of systemic discrimination, poverty, dehumanization, degendering[7] and violence. This is the punishment used against us. Importantly, though, it is also a lesson for everyone else to do everything that they can (which is obviously out of their control) not to become like us.

Under capitalism, individual productivity is linked to individual worth: the more you produce, the more money you make and the more valuable you are to society. As productivity and worth are measured entirely in monetary terms, people who are left out of the system, such as disabled people, are worthless. Of course, most disabled people who are excluded from paid labour are left out because of discrimination and inadequate workplace accommodation. Rather than arguing that disabled people can be productive in a capitalist paradigm, the radical model of disability sees capitalist values as problematic. People should not be valued by how much money we make, how much we produce or how much we contribute to an unsustainable and unjust economy.

This is not a romantic or superficial point. This is an important contribution that radical disability theory can make to radical politics today. Frequently, people who are organizing or agitating for social justice retain this core capitalist value. We often view other people's value through their contributions to the struggle, through how much work they do or how productive they are. If we truly want to create a just society, we must value people as people, not as producers.

What is considered normal or non-disabled is constructed around certain kinds of people, while leaving others out. Another myth that is firmly upheld is that disabled people are dependent and non-disabled people are independent. No one is actually independent. This is a myth perpetuated by disablism and driven by capitalism — we are all actually interdependent. Chances are, disabled or not, you don't grow all of your food. Chances are, you didn't build the car, bike, wheelchair, subway, shoes or bus that transports you. Chances are you didn't construct your home. Chances are you didn't sew your clothing (or make the fabric and thread used to sew it). The difference between the needs that many disabled people have and the needs of people who are not labelled as disabled is that non-disabled people have had their dependencies normalized. The world has been built to accommodate certain needs and call the people who need those things independent, while other needs are considered exceptional. Each of us relies on others every day. We all rely on one another for support, resources and to meet our needs. We are all interdependent. This interdependence is not weakness; rather, it is a part of our humanity.

However, disabled people are constructed as dependent and deviant rather than independent and normal. If we look at who was originally classified as disabled under the first modern categorization of disability (eugenic theory) in Western society — poor people, women, homosexuals, racialized people, physically disabled people and intellectually disabled people — the links between unproductivity and the categorization of deviance and disability are apparent. While there are clear capitalist functions for the eugenic classifications of disability, it is important to recognize that the oppression that these groups experience is not rooted solely in capitalism. Sexism, heterosexism/ homophobia, disablism and racism all exist outside of capitalism, and it would be irresponsible to argue that replacing capitalism would alleviate all oppression.

Legislative Definitions of Disability

What is constructed as disability is informed by numerous forms of oppression and has clearly changed over time. Even within a set period of time, however, definitions change depending on the intended outcome. The greater amount of access to resources and rights a piece of legislation involves, the stricter the definition becomes. Upon the examination of four legal definitions of disability that are used in the *Americans with Disabilities Act* (ADA) and Supplementary Security Income (SSI) in the United States, and the *Accessibility for Ontarians with Disabilities Act* (AODA) and Ontario Disability Support Program (ODSP) in Canada, the way that legislation and legal precedents influence social definitions of disability becomes clear.

In the United States, one of the most widespread definitions of disability is outlined in the *Americans with Disabilities Act* (1990). The ADA defines disability as "a physical or mental impairment that substantially limits one or more major life activities of such individual," and/or having a "record of," and/ or being "regarded" as, having an impairment. This definition was interesting because it diverged from the medical model, in part. It used a more rights/social model definition because it included people who were "regarded" as disabled.

However, in 1999, the U.S. Supreme Court tightened the definition of disability under the ADA. People who had "easily correctable" disabilities like nearsightedness (with glasses) or high blood pressure (with medication) were no longer considered disabled. They were told, according to Michael Bérubé (2003: 54), that they "had no basis for a suit under the ADA precisely because their disabilities were easily correctable."

This meant people filing suit under the ADA were "too disabled to be hired but somehow not disabled enough to be covered by the ADA; or, to put it this way, plaintiffs' 'easily correctable' disabilities were not so easily correctable as to allow them access to employment" (Bérubé, 2003: 54). The broad ADA definition of disability did not legally protect disabled people from discrimination because the U.S. Supreme Court found that 160 million people would be classified as disabled (54). This number was considered too high, so the definition was shifted to accommodate (wealthy) business owners rather than victims of disablist discrimination. The number of people that were able to litigate against businesses was dramatically reduced, which would limit potential liability. In order to permit fewer people the chance to access resources and accommodations, the ADA definition was made more restrictive. An amendment introduced to the ADA in 2008 was designed to refocus the definition of disability. However, peope who need to use eyeglasses continue to be exempt from the Act (Leonard, 2009), and it remains to be seen what, if any, impact the changes will actually have.

The ADA is complaint driven. Typically, an individual who has been discriminated against must have the time, energy and resources to engage in the court system to seek a remedy to the discrimination. In order to be successful, people also need evidence that is often difficult or impossible to obtain. Also, litigation requires resources — resources that many people do not have access to; however, many property owners, businesses and corporations have ample resources to defend themselves in the courts.

Further, the ADA, like the other acts I will discuss in this section, does nothing to address systemic barriers, and, while it appears to be broad and encompass a great number of people, the actual number of people who successfully pursue litigation is quite small. From July 1992 to September 2005 there were over 230,000 claims filed under the ADA for employment discrimination. Of these, roughly 33,000 (less than 15 percent) ended in favour of the complainant. Only 2.2 percent of successful claims were actually won through the courts, the rest were settled or otherwise resolved (Winegar, 2006). While this legislation has helped specific individuals remedy discrimination, its overall impact is nowhere near what is needed to undermine disablism in the United States.

Canada does not have federal disability legislation that is comparable to the ADA. The *Canadian Charter of Rights and Freedoms* (1982) protects against government discrimination on the grounds of disability (which is undefined in the law). Additionally, each province has a human rights code that contains protections for disabled people. However, human rights law does not necessarily entail physical inaccessibility or lack of interpreters, for example. Like the ADA, however, this legislation is largely complaint driven.

In Ontario, the country's most populated province, there is disability-specific legislation: the *Ontarians with Disabilities Act (ODA)* (2001). This law only requires governments to make accessibility plans, not actually to take action. In 2025, the ODA will be replaced by the *Accessibility for Ontarians with Disabilities Act* (2005) *(AODA)*, a piece of legislation much more similar to the *Americans with Disabilities Act*. The ODA and the AODA define disability as "any degree of physical disability, infirmity, malformation or disfigurement that is caused by bodily injury, birth defect or illness ... mental impairment or a developmental disability... a learning disability... [or] a mental disorder"

(*Ontarians with Disabilities Act,* 2001: 2. (1)(a); *Accessibility for Ontarians with Disabilities Act,* 2005: 2. (a)).

This definition is incredibly broad, but provides little meaningful assistance for disabled people. Additionally, the government has refused to enact the section making it an offence to break this law, so it is essentially useless — except, of course to the governing party who enacted the law, as they received extensive positive media coverage from its passage (Lepofsky, 2004).

Where the benefit to disabled people is greater and has a meaningful impact on people's lives, the definition of disability becomes much more restrictive. Supplementary Security Income (United States) and the Ontario Disability Support Program provide (measly) monthly amounts to people on disability who are declared unable to work. They both require medical documentation of conditions that are terminal or will last at least a year (Social Security Online, 2010; *Ontario Disability Support Program Act,* 1997). Disability, in the case of Supplementary Security Income (SSI), must lead to an inability "to engage in any substantial gainful activity" (Social Security Online, 2010), which to the American government means productive, paid employment. With respect to the Ontario Disability Support Program (ODSP), the definition also involves a "substantial restriction in one or more… activities of daily living," which are personal care, paid work or operating in the community (*Ontario Disability Support Program Act,* 1997: s4. (1)(c)).

Neither SSI nor ODSP account for systemic discrimination in employment; this means that there are disabled people who cannot work because they are disabled (because no one will hire them), but cannot access disability social assistance because they are not disabled under the legislated definition. The ADA and human rights legislation are supposed to remedy this, but they don't, just as civil rights legislation did not end employment discrimination on the grounds of race or racism in general. Because there is a discrepancy between who counts as disabled under the ADA and under SSI, there is a class of people who are unable to obtain employment and are unable to get income support. These people are disabled only when it is to other people's benefit, not their own.

Implications of Definitions of Disability

When people actually get access to money, accommodations, equipment or attendant care, such as those individuals defined under social assistance legislation like SSI and ODSP, the definitions of disability are rewritten, classifying very few people as disabled. But, for legislation that is general, like the ADA and, especially, the ODA, the definition is broad and aimed at reaching as many voters as possible. While there may be some benefit to being defined as disabled under certain pieces of legislation, this is primarily not to benefit *us* but rather to benefit those in power.

The same government that celebrated itself for passing the *Ontarians with Disabilities Act* arbitrarily changed the definition of disabled for social assistance, which led to thousands of people no longer being considered disabled (Toughill, 1995) and hence no longer eligible to receive financial support. Similarly, the conservative government in British Columbia redefined disability and required people receiving assistance to submit twenty-three pages of forms to re-prove they were disabled in order to retain their benefits (Lavender, 2003).[8] In the United States, the 1996 *Personal Responsibility and Work Opportunity Reconciliation Act* redefined disability, resulting in 100,000 children losing their benefits (American Academy of Pediatrics, 2001). These definitions were all made more restrictive in order to reduce benefits for many people and to save the government money.

When there is little or no benefit, but lots of stigma, to being disabled, definitions are broad. But definitions increasingly narrow as the level of and access to resources increases. These definitions, like all definitions of marginalized people, are used as forms of control, creating large groups of "others" when it is useful. Further, these definitions remain under the control of those with power and can be changed to serve their needs and desires.

Who Is Disabled?

People *are* disabled. We are disabled if those in power say we are. This is an identity that is fully out of our control. However, because it is out of our control, there are some people who are not allowed into the disability grouping because they need to access resources. By denying people the identity of disabled they are automatically refused resources, accommodations, social assistance and human rights protections. This is the plight of many people with non-apparent, or "invisible," disabilities. Further, as long as our communities remain classified in the category of disabled, rather than hold the power to create the category itself, we will have a divided disabled community, one that is unlikely to build unity and a base of resistance together. So, who is disabled? Anyone who is identified or who identifies as disabled.

As Tom Shakespeare (2006b: 77) contends, "Defining disability in terms of social barriers or social oppression, rather than a biological impairment, opens up the category to a range of other socially excluded or devalued groups." The problem with this argument is that it assumes that biological impairment and social oppression are severable, which they are not. Shakespeare takes opposition to, for example, fat people being included in the disability identity group.

However, I argue that fatness is a disability. Obesity is a medicalized condition and commonly regarded as a disability — at least depending on the definition. In *Cook v. Rhode Island Department of Mental Health, Retardation, and Hospitals* (1993), the court found that Ms. Cook was disabled under the ADA. She was a fat woman who was not hired because she was presumed to be disabled by her obesity. The ADA defines a disabled person who has, or is regarded as having, substantial limitations performing "major life activities." One of these activities is working, and Ms. Cook was unable to work because she was regarded as disabled; therefore, she was disabled under the law. This was a curtail case as *Cook* continues to have positive employment implications for fat people (Carpenter, 2006). An interesting circular definition of disability was established in this case, wherein if someone is fat and perceived to be disabled and that perception prevents them from working (or doing any of a number of other activities) then that person is disabled. This First Circuit court demonstrates what a radical understanding of disability looks like: those with power (the employer) considered someone as disabled, treated her as if she was disabled and, therefore, she was disabled.

The correlations and/or intersectionality between fatness and disablism have also been discussed by a number of authors (Aphramor, 2009; Rowen, 2006; Herndon 2002; Cooper, 1997). Like other forms of disability, the definition of and the attention paid to fatness or obesity has shifted with social values. Charlotte Cooper (1997: 33) writes, "Many fat people ... grow up fearing our own bodies in shame, public ridicule and social ostracism and the cultural fear and hatred of us can ruin our lives. I believe that self-defining as 'disabled' enables us to take ourselves seriously and demand others do also." April Herndon (2002: 122) asserts disability needs to be understood "as a diverse social category that can meaningfully incorporate fat embodiments." Cooper goes on to say, "Fat people's demands are regarded as trivial compared to those of disabled people; thus, the notion of civil rights for fat people is little more than a joke" (1997: 33).

Shakespeare and other disabled authors and activists perpetuate the trivialization of fat people's experiences and demands by their conscious exclusion of fat people from the disability umbrella. Further, as disabled people have so commonly been the brunt of the other end of this dynamic — the ones excluded, the ones who have had their oppression supported by groups trying to reduce theirs — we should not be doing the same thing to others.

Some people raise the concern that there will be people who identify as disabled who aren't actually disabled (see, for example, Shakespeare, 2006b). However, people do not claim marginality of their own choosing. There may be extreme or hypothetical circumstances in which such a situation might occur, but it doesn't make sense to exclude people based on imagined worse case scenarios. If we fail to let people self-identify as disabled, we also run the risk of legitimizing the medical model of disability, as it is the primary and oftentimes exclusive mechanism for labelling disability. Self-identification is the only way that people claim membership in the queer community and it has worked out fine. Imagine if queers were afraid that straights would start identifying as queer in order to get access to the few benefits that we have (equity hiring and awesome parties) that we made people go to a doctor to get documentation they were queer.

A parallel example of this gatekeeper phenomenon is when women-only spaces exclude trans women. This is often justified on the basis that a man could come into the space, say he is a woman and be violent. In reality, a man or a woman could come into that space and be violent. In a situation like that, which is an imagined worst-case scenario, you deal with the behaviour at the time. As someone who has done training for homeless shelters, some of which were women-only spaces, I have had this same conversation a number of times with staff and residents. For the most part, I do not think that people raise issues out of malice but out of fear. The reality is that these hypothetical situations aren't going to happen, and if they do, we can collectively deal with the situations that arise.

Further, because disablism is so deeply internalized in many disabled people, we may be hesitant to ask for accommodations. In my experience with the disabled people in my life, we don't "abuse" accommodations: we ask for fewer than we need or than would be helpful. There is a tremendous amount of stigma around disability, so disabled people are less likely to ask for what we need, not the other way around. Forcing people to prove they are disabled is not the solution to the hypothetical problem of non-disabled people saying they are disabled in order to gain advantages.

Disabled people have been overwhelmingly excluded from society. Our community shouldn't replicate the same problems. Disabled people's spaces can be empowering and important to our sense of well-being and belonging. We need to relearn ways of building community, rather than replicate the flawed divisions that have been forced on us for so long.

Difficulty and Trouble: Real Experiences of Being Disabled

Because many disabled people find pride in our disabled minds and bodies, this doesn't mean that we don't have difficulty with them. Sometimes, we do. But these difficulties are not because we are disabled; we experience them because we are human. Everyone gets frustrated with their minds and their bodies at some point. In spite of disablist discourse, this is not unique to those of us classified as disabled.

One of the key criticisms of the social model has been that it does not give space for people to talk about the difficulty that they have with their minds and bodies. Over a decade ago, Michael Oliver (1996) countered this criticism, saying that there just needed to be a social model of impairment to complement the social model of disability. However, within the hegemony of the social model, there has been an understanding that there is a separation between our political, public presentation and our private lives (Tregaskis, 2002).

To say we should just wait for a social model of impairment is simplistic and dismissive. I feel a lot of pressure from social modelists not to talk about the trouble that we have with our disability labels and our minds and bodies. I feel a responsibility to our fight for justice not to say certain things. Tom Shakespeare writes:

> Many disability rights campaigners concede that behind closed doors they talk about aches and pains and urinary tract infections, even while they deny any relevance of the body while they are out campaigning. Yet this inconsistency is surely wrong: if the public rhetoric says one thing, while everyone behaves privately in a more complete way, then perhaps it is time to re-examine the rhetoric and speak more accurately. (2006b: 52)

There is, however, a real fear for me, and I would guess the same for many others as well, to talk about my difficult experiences with my body. A few years ago, I wrote about how hard it is:

> I am afraid that I will help fuel the fires of hatred against disabled people. If I say that [my life can be painful and isolating] that could be used to support the argument that disabled people do not have full and rewarding lives. If I address the difficulty that many disabled people have accessing support and the tension that that puts on personal relationships it could be manipulated to contend that disability should be eliminated to spare parents from the burden of having a disabled child. If I talk about the depression, and even the sense of worthlessness, that can go along with chronic illness, chronic pain, and limited access it might be twisted around to bolster the position that we aren't worthy of life. If I honestly talk about the struggles that I endure on a daily basis what we have to say about our lives and the world may be reduced to inspirational material rather than meaningful and important interpretations of the world around us. (Withers, 2007: 36)

These are the secrets I have kept in order to help to build a movement. We all keep secrets.

We need to create space, within a radical theory of disability for people to talk about our difficulties. This does not mean that people who are identified as disabled necessarily have more trouble with our minds or bodies than non-disabled people. This does not mean that our difficulties are permanent or stagnant; rather, our perceptions of our minds and bodies shift depending on any number of factors.

We refuse to talk about our lives, and our troubles around them, instead of talking about them openly within a radical framework. As a result, all it takes is one Christopher Reeve (1998: 287) calling for a cure and saying "merely being alive is not enough" to reinforce the disablist notions that our arguments are wrong and our lives really are worth less, or even worthless.

Our politics cannot draw distinctions between our public and our private lives. We cannot draw arbitrary lines down our lives, leaving out parts of our lived experiences because they are not convenient to our arguments. We need a disability politic that is true to our lives, one that doesn't make us keep secrets — secrets that ultimately weaken our arguments.

Disability pride *can* co-exist with our real minds, bodies and lived experiences, which can include the joys and the difficulties that our diversity brings. Perfectly healthy people who never struggle with their minds and bodies, who are never challenged by them, do not exist. This "ideal" is a construct to perpetuate disabled people's marginalization. Evolutionary biologist Marlene Zuk argues that diseases have evolutionary purposes and are a basic presence in all of human existence. Zuk (2007: 10) cautions against a war on disease: "What we should hope for is not victory, but reconciliation." Reconciliation, with respect to disability, would mean an acceptance of human diversity, including the fact that we all have different minds, bodies, needs and abilities. It would mean welcoming the different perspectives that this diversity brings.

The kinds of people who are currently labelled disabled have always been a part of our population and offer important perspectives and contributions. Disabled people are often celebrated for our accomplishments *in spite of our disabilities* (people like Franklin Roosevelt and Helen Keller). We are rarely recognized for the contributions we make *because of our disabilities*. For instance, when I am having a hard time walking, I walk very slowly and I notice a lot of what is around me. Because I experience the world differently than many of the people around me, I have a unique and useful perspective.

Radical Access

Within the disability rights and social models, accessibility means different things depending on who you are talking to and when you are talking to them. Ideas of accessibility were often more restricted and solely focused on physical access (i.e., lifts and ramps) in decades past, but the ideas surrounding access have begun to expand.

Like all disability models coming from disabled people, one of the key issues is access. However, the radical model does not advocate solely for ramps and lifts — though physical accommodations should always be present. We advocate and agitate for radical access. Access needs to be addressed collectively, across bodies, boundaries and borders. Radical access means acknowledging systemic barriers that exclude people, particularly certain kinds of people with certain kinds of minds and/or bodies, and working to ensure not only the presence of those who have been left out, but also their comfort, participation and leadership. Spaces that need to incorporate radical access principles are organizational, they are educational and institutional, but they are also the spaces closest to us: our cafés, our offices, our homes and our hearts.

Radical access is not about "universal design" or universal access — that is an arbitrary and fictional concept. According to Ron Mace, the man who coined the term "universal design," it is "the design of products and environments to be usable by all people, to the greatest extent possible, without the need for adaptation or specialized design" (Center for Universal Design, n.d.). The problem with this concept is that people and their needs change. An obvious, and unfair, example is that if a building that fits a universal design or access mould is in Finland and I cannot go to Finland, then it isn't accessible to me. However, even if the building is downtown, but transit is expensive and I don't have the money, or if I am a Black man and the streetcar refuses to stop to let me on, or if I am a wheelchair user and the streetcar is not physically accessible to me, that building is not universally accessible. Access doesn't just begin at the front door.

When I was much younger and was relatively new to activism, I frequently talked about identity groups exclusively as groups, not about the many individual people who make up those groups. One of the most valuable things that developing the radical disability model and radical access politics have taught me is that I cannot simply paint groups with one brush. Access politics demand that we treat people as people and look at each of our needs and how to collectively meet them. While there are specific, basic demands that we need to put in place to ensure some standards of accessibility, each of us has our own needs, and access should be collectively negotiated between everyone involved. This negotiation is never neutral and cannot take place without considering present-day oppression, as well as the histories of oppression. This negotiation is not about creating room for people in spite of their marginality but recognizing that everyone deserves space and that their membership in an oppressed group brings perspectives and experiences that are not only welcome but wanted.

Radical access also includes intentional and accessible use of language. This means that one strives to communicate in ways that are easily understood. It also means that oppressive language is not used. This includes disablist language, which is pervasive within North America and the Left. Sometimes, however, words do have multiple meanings according to the dictionary: "paralyze" can mean to fully stop; "deaf" can mean to refuse to listen; "disable" can mean to break or turn off; and "crazy "can mean ridiculous. But, as Chris Chapman says, while these words "have acceptable usages about things other than people, in terms of what dictionaries say, I would suggest that it is impossible to use these words without evoking people." Chapman (2010, n.p.) argues that "whatever dictionaries say — it would be impossible for me to say 'gay' and have it only signify 'happy.'" Double usage or not, disablist slurs need to be stripped out of everyday language if we want to create spaces where disabled people feel welcome and wanted. No space is ever accessible if oppressive language is being used, no matter what other measures are taken to make it so.

Conclusion

This model would not have been possible to imagine before the disability rights movement, the social model or the important work of many radical activists and thinkers. There are also many directions this model could go in. For example, there could be important shifts in language. For instance, the term disability justice is used, largely on the West Coast of the United States, to radically respond to the disability rights movement. Also, a disabled friend of mine, Amanda Dorter, has started using the word "disablized" to talk about disabled people in order to better indicate the imposition of the disability label. As people begin to see themselves, and others, in increasingly radical ways, our politics and the words that we use to talk about them will evolve.

It is important, however, that the fundamental tenets of the model — the necessity of recognizing and relating to intersectionality, that disability is a social construction, that the disability label is imposed as a tactic to retain power and social control and that we have to create space for each other both in terms of acknowledging our lived experiences and ensuring accessibility — remain intact. Rather than perpetuating unrealistic ideals for humans, radical disability theory calls for reassessing and revaluing people. We should not be penalized for falling outside of arbitrary and unjust norms of productivity and independence. There is nothing wrong with us. We should be celebrated for our diversities and our perspectives.

Radical access and radical disability theory are not fringe ideas — they are fundamental ideas looking at the essence of what disability and access mean for everyone. Radical disability theory is about fighting to redistribute power and resources and creating accessible spaces and communities.

By fighting to make it happen, I literally mean that we have to fight. Radical access and an end to disablism will never be handed to us. We have to work together to demand and create change. We have to move beyond the identity politic of physical access and work to create access for all. We have to constantly and consistently confront our own actions and ways of reinforcing oppression. Perhaps most importantly though, we must organize. We must work in solidarity with other marginalized groups, and we must get past our differences and fight for justice, dignity, equality and access.

Notes

1. While I am putting this theory forward, it was collectively developed, particularly with Loree Erickson. Griffin Epstein has also been integral to its articulation, especially that of radical access.
2. I have avoided including anthologies or books that contain a number of chapters and discuss multiple oppressions because this frequently amounts to tokenism, rather than inclusion or intersectionality. The same is true of a work that minimally talks about intersectionality.
3. This particular reference is in relation to inclusion in schools.
4. Early mainstream gay rights activists did not just work to establish themselves as non-disabled, but also as non-racialized. Like first-wave and second-wave feminists, mainstream gay rights activists erased the plethora of racial and cultural diversity from their populations to gain access to privileges for the white people within that identity group. Its leadership actively upheld that homosexuals were more oppressed than African Americans. Kameny (1965: 12) said: "In this country an individual known to be a homosexual would find it more difficult to get an education, at any level, in the school of his choice (or, in fact, in any school at all) — than would a Negro in the South." This statement, while likely false, failed to acknowledge Black queers and trivializes the struggles of Blacks in the South. The early mainstream movement also presented a specific class and gender role image of homosexuals. Demonstrations required that participants follow a dress code, requiring gender appropriate business attire (Alwood, 1996; Kissack, 1995).
5. The gay liberation movement, as opposed to the mainstream gay rights movement, did have an anti-racist, anti-sexist, anti-war, anti-consumerist, if not anti-capitalist platform (Rimmerman, 2008).
6. A notable exception to this pattern in public transit campaigns by disabled people is that of DAMN, a radical disability organization in Toronto. DAMN has campaigned for accessible transit for all using a radical access approach rather than a disability rights approach.
7. Frequently, disabled people are seen as non-gendered or our disabilities are understood as our genders.
8. Later, this was changed so people with certain diagnoses did not have to do it.

References

Abbott, Anne. 2011. Personal interview. Toronto, August 27.

Accessibility for Ontarians with Disabilities Act. 2005. S.O. 2005, Chapter 11, last amendment: 2009, c. 33, Sched. 8, s. 3.

Ad Punch. 2007. "Metlife Foundation: Alzheimer's Disease Steals Normal Life." <adpunch.org/entry/metlife-foundation-alzheimers-disease-steals-normal-life>.

Adelson, Betty M. 2005. *Dwarfism: Medical and Psychosocial Aspects of Profound Short Stature.* Baltimore: Johns Hopkins University Press.

Ahmad, Waqar I.U. 2000. "Introduction." In Waqar I.U. Ahmad (ed.), *Ethnicity, Disability and Chronic Illness.* Buckingham: Open University Press.

Alibey v. Canada (Minister of Citizenship and Immigration). 2004 FC 305.

Alland, Alexander Jr., Michael L. Blakey, C. Loring Brace, Alan H. Goodman, Stephen Molnar, J. Phillippe Rushton, Vincent M. Sarich and Audrey Smedley. 1996. "Review: The Eternal Triangle: Race, Class and IQ." *Current Anthropology* 37, S1 (February).

Alwood, Edward. 1996. *Straight News: Gays, Lesbians, and the News Media.* New York: Columbia University Press.

American Academy of Pediatrics. 2001. "The Continued Importance of Supplemental Security Income (SSI) for Children and Adolescents With Disabilities." *Pediatrics* 107, 4 (April). <aappolicy.aappublications.org/cgi/content/abstract/pediatrics;107/4/790>.

American Cancer Society. 2010. *A Defining Moment: Annual Report 2010.* <cancer.org/AboutUs/WhoWeAre/AnnualReport/2010-annual-report>.

American Institute of Philanthropy. 2010. *Top 25 Compensation Packages.* <charitywatch.org/hottopics/Top25>.

American Psychiatric Association. 2000. *Diagnostic and Statistical Manual of Mental Disorders: DSM-IV-TR.* Washington, DC: Psychiatryonline. <psychiatryonline.com>.

Americans with Disabilities Act of 1990 (ADA) 104 Stat. 327, 42 USC § 12101 et seq.

Aphramor, Lucy. 2009. "Disability and the Anti-Obesity Offensive." *Disability and Society* 24, 7.

Arad, Yitzhak. 1987. *Belzec, Sobibor, Treblinka: The Operation Reinhard Death Camps.* Bloomington: Indiana University Press [1999].

Arthritis Society. n.d. <arthritis.ca/arthritis%20home/default.asp?s=1>.

Ashby, Chris. 2010. "The Trouble with Normal: The Struggle for Meaningful Access for Middle School Students with Developmental Disability Labels." *Disability and Society* 25, 3.

Aszuba and Salvation Army Sheltered Workshop et al. [1983] O.J. No. 2982.

Badinter, Elisabeth. 1992. In Lydia Davis (trans.) *XY: On Masculine Identity*. New York: Colombia University Press [1995].

Baldwin, Steve, and Yvonne Jones. 1998. "Is Electroconvulsive Therapy Unsuitable for Children and Adolescents?" *Adolescence* 33, 131 (Fall).

Banton, Martin, and Gurnam Singh. 2004. "'Race,' Disability and Oppression." In John Swain, Sally French, Colin Barnes and Carol Thomas (eds.), *Disabling Barriers, Enabling Environments*. 2nd ed. London: Sage.

Barnes, Colin, Geof Mercer and Tom Shakespeare. 1999. *Exploring Disability: A Sociological Introduction*. Malden, MA: Blackwell Publishing.

Barnett, J., and S. Hammond.1999. "Representing Disability in Charity Promotions." *Journal of Community and Applied Social Psychology* 9, 4 (July).

Barone, Michael J., Anthony D. Miyazaki and Kimberly A. Taylor. 2000. "The Influence of Cause-Related Marketing on Consumer Choice: Does One Good Turn Deserve Another?" *Journal of the Academy of Marketing Science* 28, 2.

Bascaramurty, Dakshana. 2010. "Guilt Giving: Will You Cave at the Register?" *Globe and Mail*, December 14. <www.theglobeandmail.com/globe-investor/personal-finance/putting-the-touch-on-you-at-the-checkout/article1836609/>.

Baynton, Douglas. 2002. "Beyond Culture: Deaf Studies and the Deaf Body." In H. Dirksen and L. Bauman (eds.), *Open Your Eyes: Deaf Studies Talking*. Minneapolis: University of Minnesota Press [2008].

____. 2001. "Disability and the Justification of Inequality in American History." In Paul Longmore and Lauri Umansky (eds.), *The New Disability History: American Perspectives*. New York: New York University Press.

Beckwith, Jon. 1993. "A Historical View of Social Responsibility in Genetics." *Bioscience* 43, 5 (May).

Being Physically Disabled Does Not Automatically Make Us Stupid. n.d. Facebook. <www.facebook.com/group.php?gid=2304422816#!/group.php?gid=2304422816&v=wall>

Bell, Chris. 2010. "Is Disability Studies Actually White Disability Studies?" In Lennard J. Davis (ed.), *Disability Studies Reader*. New York: Routledge.

Benjamin, Akua. 2005. "Response." In Paul K. Longmore. "The Hand That Feeds... Charity Telethons and Disability Activism." Ryerson University, November 11. <ryecast.ryerson.ca/dmpstreams/rbc2005/index.asp>.

Benjoe, Kerry. 2010. "Buy an Egg to Help Send a Kid to Camp." *Regina Leader Post*, March 9.

Beresford, Peter. 2004. "Madness, Distress, Research and a Social Model." In Colin Barnes and Geof Mercer (ed.), *Implementing the Social Model of Disability: Theory and Research*. Leeds: The Disability Press.

Beresford, P., G. Gifford and C. Harrison. 1996. "What Has Disability Got to Do with Psychiatric Survivors?" In J. Reynolds and J. Read (eds.), *Speaking Our Minds: an Anthology of Personal Experience of Mental Distress and its Consequences*. San Diego: DawnSighPress.

Berglind, Matthew, and Cheryl Nakata. 2005. "Cause-Related Marketing: More Buck than Bang?" *Business Horizons* 48, 5 (September–0October).

Bérubé, Michael. 2003. "Citizenship and Disability." *Dissent* 50, 2 (Spring).

Bethlehem, Douglas W. 1985. *A Social Psychology of Prejudice*. Beckneham: Croom Helm.

Bhanushali, Kishor. 2007. "Changing Face of Disability Movement: From Charity to Empowerment." *National Seminar on "Revisiting Social Work in the field of Health — A Journey from Welfare to Empowerment*. Maharaja Sayjirao University of Baroda, Vadodara, February 20–21. <handicap-international.fr/bibliographie-handicap/6SocieteCivile/Autonomisation/Changing_Face_of_Disability_Movement_From_Charity_to_Empowerment.pdf>.

Biesold, Horst. 1999. In William Sayers (trans.), *Crying Hands: Eugenics and Deaf People in Nazi Germany*. Washington D.C.: Gallaudet University Press.

Black, Edwin. 2003. *War Against The Weak: Eugenics and America's Campaign to Create a Master Race*. New York: Four Walls Eight Windows.

Blackwell, Tom. 2003. "Doctor to Pay $200,000 in 'Wrongful Birth' Suit." *National Post*, Jan. 30.

Blake, Sarah J. 2002. "Beating Blindisms." *See/Hear* 7, 2 (Spring).

Bleir, Ruth. 1984. *Science and Gender: A Critique of Biology and Its Theories of Women*. New York: Pergamon Press.

Boyce, William Mary Tremblay, Mary Anne McColl, Jerome Birckenbach, Ann Crichton, Steven Andrews, Nancy Gerein, and April D'Aubin. 2001. *A Seat at the Table: Persons with Disabilties and Policy Making*. Montreal: McGill-Queen's University Press.

Brady, Shelly. 2002. *Ten Things I Learned from Bill Porter: The Inspiring True Story of the Door-to-Door Salesman Who Changed Lives*. Novato, CA: New World Library.

Braslow, Joel T. 1997. *Mental Ills and Bodily Cures: Psychiatric Treatment in the First Half of the Twentieth Century*. Berkeley: University of California Press.

Broc Glover's Breathe Easy Ride Against Cystic Fibrosis. 2009. *Dirt Bike Magazine* March 4. <www.dirtbikemagazine.com/ME2/dirmod.asp?sid=&nm=&type=news&mod=News&mid=9A02E3B96F2A415ABC72CB5F516B4C10&tier=3&nid=E247FFD74BAA4C4AA838F1FAB355C526>.

Bronski, Michael. 1984. *Culture Clash: The Making of Gay Sensibility*. Boston: South End Press.

Brown, Keith, Doris Hammer, Susan Foley and Jonathan Woodring. 2009. "Doing Disability: Disability Formations in the Search for Work." *Sociological Inquiry* 79,1 (February).

Buck v. Bell. 1927. 274 U.S. 200.

Burstow, Bonnie. 2006. "Electroshock as a Form of Violence Against Women." *Violence Against Women* 12, 4 (April).

Burstow, Bonnie, and Don Weitz. 1988. "Introduction." In Bonnie Burstow and Don Weitz (eds.), *Shrink Resistant: The Struggle Against Psychiatry in Canada*. Vancouver: New Star Books.

Butler, Amos W. 1921. "Some Families as Factors in Anti-Social Conditions." *Eugenics, Genetics and Family: 2nd International Congress of Eugenics, V.1*. New York: Garland Publishing [1984].

Butler, Judith. 1999. *Gender Trouble: Feminism and the Subversion of Identity.* New York: Routledge.

Butterworth, John, Allison Hall, David Hoff and Alberto Migliore. 2007. *State and International Efforts to Reform or Eliminate the Use of Sub-Minimum Wage for Persons with Disabilities.* Boston: Institute for Community Inclusion, University of Boston.

Campbell, Fiona A. Kumari. 2008. "Exploring Internalized Ableism Using Critical Race Theory." *Disability and Society* 23, 2.

Campbell, Jane, and Mike Oliver. 1996. *Disability Politics: Understanding Our Past, Changing Our Future.* London: Routledge.

Canada Revenue Agency. 2011. "Schedule 3: Compensation — Muscular Dystrophy Canad/ Dystrophie Musculaire Canada." <www.cra-arc.gc.ca/ebci/haip/srch/ t3010form21sched3-eng.action?b=107755837RR0001&e=2010-03-31&n=M USCULAR+DYSTROPHY+CANADA+%2F+DYSTROPHIE+MUSCULAIR E+CANADA&r=http%3A%2F%2Fwww.cra-arc.gc.ca%3A80%2Febci%2Fhaip% 2Fsrch%2Ft3010form21-eng.action%3Fb%3D107755837RR0001%26amp%3B e%3D2010-03-31%26amp%3Bn%3DMUSCULAR%2BDYSTROPHY%2BCA NADA%2B%252F%2BDYSTROPHIE%2BMUSCULAIRE%2BCANADA%26a mp%3Br%3Dhttp%253A%252F%252Fwww.cra-arc.gc.ca%253A80%252Febci% 252Fhaip%252Fsrch%252Fbasicsearchresult-eng.action%253Fs%253Dregistere d%2526amp%253Bk%253Dmuscular%252Bdystrophy%2526amp%253Bp%25 3D1%2526amp%253Bb%253Dtrue>.

Canadian Association of Genetic Counselors. n.d. "Canadian Medical Genetics Clinics." <cagc-accg.ca/component/option,com_sobi2/Itemid,30/>.

Canadian Cancer Society. 2011. "Bottom-line Benefits." <cancer.ca/Canada-wide/How you can help/CW-Corporate giving/CW-Bottom-line benefits.aspx?sc_lang=en>.

____. 2010. "End-of-life Care and the Canadian Cancer Society." <www.cancer.ca/ Canada-wide/About us/Media centre/CW-Media releases/CW-2010/End-of-life Care and the Canadian Cancer Society.aspx?sc_lang=en".

____. 2009–2010. *Join The Fight!* <annualreport.cancer.ca/#>.

Canadian Charter of Rights and Freedoms, Part I of the *Constitution Act,* 1982, being Schedule B to the *Canada Act 1982* (U.K.), Chapter 11.

Canadian Cystic Fibrosis Foundation. n.d. "Why Do People Volunteer?" <cysticfibrosis. ca/en/getInvolved/WhyDoPeopleVolunteer.php>.

Canadian Institute for Mental Health Information. 2011. "Nearly One in Four Mental Health Inpatients in Ontario Experiences Some form of Restraint or Seclusion." August 23. <www.cihi.ca/CIHI-ext-portal/internet/en/Document/ types+of+care/specialized+services/mental+health+and+addictions/ RELEASE_23AUG11?WT.ac=homepage_banner_20110823_e>.

Canadian Press. 2006. "Que. Doctors Lagging in Fee-For-Service Payments." CTV *News,* December 21. <ctv.ca/CTVNews/Canada/20061221/quebec_doctors_061221/>.

____. 1998. "Push to Eliminate Genetic Disease may not Be Desirable: Professor [Dick Sobsey]." *Canadian Press NewsWire,* September 13.

Canadian Women's Committee on Reproduction, Population and Development. 1995.

"Canadian Policies and Practices in the Areas of Reproduction, Population and Development." *Canadian Women Studies* 15, 2/3 (Spring/Summer).

Carlson, Licia. 2010. *The Faces of Intellectual Disability: Philosophical Reflections.* Bloomington: Indiana University Press.

Carpenter, Christopher S. 2006. "The Effects of Employment Protection for Obese People." *Industrial Relations: A Journal of Economy & Society* 45, 3 (July).

CBC News. 2007. "Mills Praised as 'Inspiration' in Dancing With the Stars Debut." March 20. < www.cbc.ca/arts/tv/story/2007/03/20/dancing-stars-mills. html#ixzz0xAw26zSB>.

Center for Universal Design. n.d. NC State University. <design.ncsu.edu/cud/about_ud/about_ud>.

Chapman, Chris. 2010. "Crippling Narratives and Disabling Shame: Disability as a Metaphor, Affective Dividing Practices, and an Ethics that Might Make a Difference." *The Space Between: Disability in and out of the Counselling Room,* conference, Toronto, OISE, University of Toronto, October 8.

Chee, Re (1905), 11 B.C.R. 400. Quicklaw.

Chester, Phyllis. 2005. *Women and Madness.* Revised edition. Houndmills: Palgrave Macmillan.

Christopher and Dana Reeve Foundation. n.d. "Join Team Reeve." <christopherreeve. org/site/c.ddJFKRNoFiG/b.4452251/k.39D9/Who_Are_the_Team_Reeve_All_Stars.htm>.

CIBC Run for the Cure Canadian Breast Cancer Foundation. n.d. Pamphlet.

Clare, Eli. 2009. *Exile and Pride: Disability, Queerness and Liberation.* Classics Edition. Cambridge: South End Press.

____. 2001. "Stolen Bodies, Reclaimed Bodies: Disability and Queerness." *Public Culture* 13, 3 (Fall).

____. 1999. *Exile and Pride: Disability, Queerness and Liberation.* Cambridge: South End Press.

Cohen v. Canada (Minister of Citizenship & Immigration). (2006). 55 Imm. L.R. (3d) 21.

Cone, Carol L., Mark A. Feldman, and Alison T. DaSilva. 2003. Causes and Effects. *Harvard Business Review* 81, 7 (July).

Conrad, Peter. 2007. *The Medicalization of Society: On the Transformation of Human Conditions into Treatable Disorders.* Baltimore: Johns Hopkins University Press.

Cook v. Rhode Island Department of Mental Health, Retardation, and Hospitals. 1993. USCA First Circuit No. 93-1093.

Cooper, Charlotte. 1997. "Can a Fat Woman Call Herself Disabled?" *Disability & Society* 12, 1.

Cooper, Chet. n.d.a. "Bree Walker Interviewed by Chet Cooper." *ABILITY Magazine.* <abilitymagazine.com/walker_interview.html>.

____. n.d.b. "The Road I Have Taken: Christopher Reeve and the Cure; An Interview with Christopher Reeve and Fred Fay, PhD by ABILITY Magazine's Editor-in-Chief Chet Cooper." *ABILITY Magazine.* <abilitymagazine.com/reeve_interview.html>.

Cooper, Davina. 2009. *Intersectionality and Beyond: Law, Power and the Politics of Location.* New York: Routledge-Cavendish.

Council of Canadians with Disabilities (CCD). n.d. "About CCD." <ccdonline.ca/en/about>.

Crow, Liz. 1996. "Including All of Our Lives: Renewing the Social Model of Disability." In Jenny Morris (ed.), *Encounters with Strangers: Feminism and Disability*. London: Women's Press.

Cystic Fibrosis Canada. 2010. *Higher and Higher: 2010 Annual Report*. <cysticfibrosis.ca/assets/files/pdf/AnnualReport10E.pdf>.

Cystic Fibrosis Foundation. 2010. *Hope In Our Hands: Cystic Fibrosis Foundation 2010 Annual Report*. <cff.org/UploadFiles/aboutCFFoundation/AnnualReport/2010-Annual-Report.pdf>.

Czerniawski, Amanda M. 2007. "From Average to Ideal: The Evolution of the Height and Weight Table in the United States, 1836–1943." *Social Science History* 31, 2 (Summer).

D'Aubin, April. 2003. "We Will Ride." In Deborah Stienstra and Aileen Wight-Felske (eds.), *Making Equality: History of Advocacy and People With Disabilities in Canada*. Concord, ON: Captus Press.

Dahl, Melissa. 2008. "Shock Therapy Makes a Quiet Comeback." MSNBC June 8. <msnbc.msn.com/id/26044935/>.

Darwin, Leonard. 1926. *The Need for Eugenic Reform*. New York: Garland Publishing [1984].

Davenport, Charles B. 1912a. "The Family-History Book." *Eugenics Record Office Bulletin* 7 (September).

____. 1912b. "Marriage Laws and Customs." *Problems in Eugenics: 1st International Eugenics Congress Volume 1*. New York: Garland Publishing, 1984.

Davidson, Kirk. 2003. *Selling Sin: The Marketing of Socially Unacceptable Products*. Westport, CT: Praeger Publishers.

Davis, Angela. 1990. "Racism, Birth Control, and Reproductive Rights." In Marlene Gerber Fried (ed.), *From Abortion to Reproductive Freedom: Transforming a Movement*. Boston: South End Press 1990.

Davis, Lennard J. 2002. *Bending Over Backwards: Disability, Dismodernism, and Other Difficult Positions*. New York: New York University Press.

____. 1995. *Enforcing Normalcy: Disability, Deafness and the Body*. New York: Verso.

Defeat Diabetes Foundation Inc. <defeatdiabetes.org>.

Devereaux, Cecily. 2005. *Crowing a Race: Nellie L. McClung and the Fiction of Eugenic Feminism*. Montreal: McGill-Queen's University Press.

Devlieger, Patrick, Frank Rusch and David Pfeiffer. 2003. "Toward a Cultural Model of Disability." In Patrick Devlieger, Frank Rusch and David Pfeiffer (eds.), *Rethinking Disability: The Emergence of New Definitions, Concepts and Communities*. Antwerpen: Garant.

Diller, Matthew. 2000. "Judicial Backlash, the ADA, and the Civil Rights Model." *Berkeley Journal of Employment and Labor Law* 21, 1.

Doddington K., R.S.P. Jones and B.Y. Miller. 1994. "Are Attitudes to People with Learning Disabilities Negatively Influenced by Charity Advertising?" *Disability & Society* 9, 2

Doe v. Bell. 2003. SCNY, 194 Misc. 2d 774.

Dossa, Parin. 2009. *Racialized Bodies, Disabling Worlds: Storied Lives of Immigrant Muslim Women.* Toronto: University of Toronto Press.

Dowling, Colette. 2000. *The Frailty Myth: Redefining the Physical Potential of Women and Girls.* New York: Random House Trade Paperbacks [2001].

Duff, Raymond, and A.G.M. Campbell. 1997. "Moral and Ethical Dilemmas in the Special-Care Nursery." In Nancy S. Jecker, Albert R. Jonsen, and Robert A. Pearlman (eds.), *Bioethics: An Introduction to the History, Methods and Practice.* Sudbury, Ma: Jones and Bartlett Publishers.

Dully, Howard, and Charles Fleming. 2007. *My Lobotomy: A Memoir.* New York: Three Rivers Press, 2008.

E. (D.) v. R., 2003 BCSC 1013.

E. (Mrs.) v. Eve, [1986] 2 S.C.R. 388.

East, Edward M. 1919. *Inbreeding and Outbreeding: Their Genetic and Sociological Significance.* Philadelphia: Washington Square Press.

Easter Seals. 2009–2010. *2009–2010 Annual Report.* <easterseals.com/site/SocServer/ ES_AR10_1_.pdf?docID=141507>.

____.n.d.a. "The Story of Easter Seals." <easterseals.com/site/PageServer?pagename=ntl_ wwa_we_are>.

____. n.d.b. "Watch My Movie." <easterseals.com/site/PageServer?pagename=ntl_ torimovie_homepage1>.

Easter Seals Canada. 2009–2010. *Easter Seals Canada: Annual Report 2009/10.* <easterseals.ca/English/wp-content/uploads/2011/06/AR-09_10-FINAL.pdf>.

____. n.d. <easterseals.ca/English>.

Eayrs, Caroline B., Nick Ellis, Robert S.P. Jones and Beth Miller 1994. "Representations of Learning Disability in the Literature of Charity Campaigns." In Ivana Markova and Robert M. Farr (eds.), *Representations of Health, Illness and Handicap.* New York: Harwood Academic.

Ehrenreich, Barbara, and Deirdre English. 1976. *Complaints and Disorders: The Sexual Politics of Sickness.* Westbury, NY: Feminist Press.

Ehrlichman, John. 1982. *Witness to Power: The Nixon Years.* New York: Simon and Schuster.

Elfenbein, Daniel W., and Briand McManus. 2010. "A Greater Price for a Greater Good? Evidence that Consumers Pay More for Charity-Linked Products." *American Economic Journal: Economic Policy* 2, 2 (May).

Elliott, Timothy R., and Laura Dreer. 2007. "Disability." In Susan Ayers et al. (eds.), *Cambridge Handbook of Psychology, Health and Medicine.* 2nd ed. Cambridge: Cambridge University Press.

Ellis, Albert, Mike Abrams and Lidia Dengelegi Abrams. 2009. *Personality Theories: Critical Perspectives.* Thousand Oaks, CA: Sage.

Emmett, Tony. 2006. "Disability, Poverty, Gender and Race." In Brian Watermeyer, Leslie Swartz, Theresa Lorenzo, Marguerite Schneider and Mark Preistley (eds.), *Disability and Social Change: The South African Agenda.* Cape Town: HSRC Press.

Enbridge Ride to Conquer Cancer. n.d. <conquercancer.ca/index>.

Engs, Ruth Clifford. 2000. *Clean Living Movements: American Cycles of Health Reform*. Westport: Greenwood (2001).

Enns, Ruth. 1999. *A Voice Unheard: The Latimer Case and People With Disabilities*. Halifax: Fernwood.

Entman, Robert M. 2006. *Young Men of Color in the Media: Images and Impacts*. Washington DC: Joint Center Health Policy Institute Background Paper. <jointcenter.org/publications1/publication-PDFs/Dellums%20PDFs/RobertEntman.pdf>.

Epstein, Griffin. 2011. Personal interview. Toronto, July 18.

____. 2009. "Extension: Towards a Genealogical Accountability (The Critical [E] raci[ing] of Mad Jewish Identity." Unpublished thesis, OISE, University of Toronto.

Erevelles, Nirmala Anne Kanga, and Renee Middleton. 2006. "How Does It Feel to Be a Problem? Race, Disability and Exclusion in Educational Policy." In Ellen A. Brantlinger (ed.), *Who Benefits From Special Education?: Remediating (Fixing) Other People's Children*, Mahwah, NJ: Lawrence Erlbaum Associates [2008].

Erickson, Loree. 2011. Personal interview. Toronto, August 25.

____. 2010. Personal interview. Toronto, August 13.

____. 2007. "Revealing Femmegimp: A Sex-positive Reflection on Sites of Shame and Sites of Resistance for People with Disabilities." *Atlantis* 31, 2.

Evans, Suzanne E. 2004. *Forgotten Crimes: The Holocaust and People with Disabilities*. Chicago: Ivan R. Dee.

Ewen, Stewart. 1976. *Captains of Consciousness: Advertising and the Social Roots of the Consumer*. New York: McGraw-Hill.

Exciteddelirium.org. n.d. "What is Excited Delirium?" <exciteddelirium.org/index-whatisED2.html>.

Fairchild, A.L., and E.A. Tynan. 1994. "Policies of Containment: Immigration in the Era of AIDS." *American Journal of Public Health* 84,12 (Decembwe).

Federal, Provincial and Territorial Advisory Committee on Population Health. 1999. *Toward a Healthy Future: Second Report on the Health of* Canadians." Prepared for the Meeting of Ministers of Health, Charlettetown, P.E.I.

Fenton v. Forensic Psychiatric Services Commission 1991-05-31 BCCA V01130.

Filc, D. 2004. "The Medical Text: Between Biomedicine and Hegemony." *Social Science & Medicine* 59, 6 (September).

Fine, Michelle, and Adrienne Asch (eds.). 1988. *Women with Disabilities: Essays in Psychology, Culture, and Politics* Philadelphia: Temple University Press.

Finger, Anne. 1987. "And the Greatest of These Is Charity." In Barrett Shaw (ed.), *The Ragged Edge: The Disability Experience from the Pages of the First Fifteen Years of the Disability Rag*. Louisville: Avocado Press [1994].

Finkelstein, Vic. 2001. "The Social Model of Disability Repossessed." Manchester Coalition of Disabled People. <www.leeds.ac.uk/disability-studies/archiveuk/finkelstein/soc mod repossessed.pdf>.

____. 1993. "Disability: A Social Challenge or an Administrative Responsibility." In John Swain, Vic Finkelstein, Sally French and Mike Oliver (eds.), *Disabling Barriers, Enabling Environments*. London: Sage.

____. 1990. "Conductive Education: A Tale of Two Cities." *Therapy Weekly* March 22. <http://www.leeds.ac.uk/disability-studies/archiveuk/finkelstein/A%20 Tale%20of%20Two%20Cities.pdf>.

Foucault, Michele. 1969. *Archeology of Knowledge*. London: Routledge. 2002.

Foundation Fighting Blindness. n.d. <ffb.ca>.

Fowler, Joanne, et al. 2008. "Heroes of the Year." *People Weekly* 70, 21 (Nov. 24).

Frazier, Mya. 2007. "Bono & Co. Spend up to $100 Mil on Marketing, Incur Watchdogs' Wrath." *Advertising Age* 78, 10 (March 5).

Friedman, Saul S. 2004. *A History of the Holocaust*. Portland: Mitchell Vallentine.

Galton, David J., and Clare J. Galton. 1998. "Francis Galton: and Eugenics Today." *Journal of Medical Ethics* 24, 2.

Galton, Francis. 1907. *Inquiries into Human Faculty and its Development*. 2nd ed. London: J.M. Dent & Sons.

Garber, Mark A., George Bergus, Jeffrey Dawson, G. Blake Wood, Barcey T. Levy, Irwin Levin. 2000. "Effect of a Patient's Psychiatric History on Physicians' Estimation of Probability of Disease." *Journal of General Internal Medicine* 15, 3 (March).

Garland-Thomson, Rosemarie. 2005. "Feminist Disability Studies: A Review Essay." *Signs: Journal of Women in Culture and Society* 30, 2 (Winter).

____. 2002. "Integrating Disability, Transforming Feminist Theory." *NWSA Journal* 14, 3.

____. 1994. "Redrawing the Boundaries of Feminist Disability Studies." *Feminist Studies* 20, 3 (Fall).

Gerhart, Kenneth A., Jane Koziol-McLain, Steven Rlowenstein and Gale G. Whiteneck. 1994. "Quality of Life Following Spinal Cord Injury: Knowledge and Attitudes of Emergency Care Providers." *Annals of Emergency Medicine* 23, 4 (April).

German, Beric. 2009. Worker's Assembly Public Meeting.Toronto, October 2.

GID Reform Advocates. 2005. "Why Are GID Issues Needlessly Divisive?" In Dan Karasic and Jack Drescher (eds.). <www.transgender.org/gidr/>.

Gill, Carol. 2000. "Health Professionals, Disability, and Assisted Suicide: An Examination of Relevant Empirical Evidence and Reply to Batvia (2000)." *Psychology, Public Policy and Law* 6, 2 (June).

____. 1994. "Questioning Continuum." In Barrett Shaw (ed.), *The Ragged Edge: The Disability Experience from the Pages of the First Fifteen Years of the Disability Rag*. Louisville: Avocado Press.

Gill, Carol, J., Kristi L.Kirschner and Judith Panko Reis. 1994. "Health Services for Women with Disabilities: Barriers and Portals. Reframing Women's Health: Multidisciplinary Research and Practice." In Alice J. Dan (ed.), *Reframing Women's Health: Multidisciplinary Research and Practice*. Thousand Oaks, CA: Sage Publications

Gill, Michael. 2005. "The Myth of Transition: Contractualizing Disability in the Sheltered Workshop." *Disability & Society* 20, 6.

Gillis, Charlie. 2001. "Not Welcome: For Generations, Canada Has Restricted Immigration to the Healthy and Able, Preserving the Nation's Health Care Services from the World's Sick and Needy." *National Post*, March 30.

Gindin, Sam. 2002. "Capitalism and the Terrain of Social Justice." *Monthly Review* 53,

09 (February). <monthlyreview.org/2002/02/01/capitalism-and-the-terrain-of-social-justice>.

Gleeson, Brendan. 1999. *Geographies of Disability*. New York: Routledge.

Goodley, Dan. 2011. *Disability Studies: An Interdisciplinary Introduction*. Thousand Oaks, CA: Sage Publications.

Goodwin, Donna L., and Kerri Staples. 2005. "The Meaning of Summer Camp Experiences to Youths with Disabilities." *Adapted Physical Activity Quarterly* 22, 2 (April).

Greger, Michael. 1999. "Me and My Ego-Alien Oral Cannibalistic Impulses." *Heart Failure: Diary of a Third Year Medical Student*. <upalumni.org/medschool/appendices/appendix-42.html on>.

Grekul, Jana. 2008. "Sterilization in Alberta, 1928–1982: Gender Matters." *Canadian Review of Sociology* 45, 3 (August).

Grey Group Canada. n.d. "Special Olympics Canada." <www.grey.com/canada/index.html?section=HOME&sid=TORONTO>.

Groce, Nora Ellen. 1985. *Everyone Here Spoke Sign Language: Hereditary Deafness on Martha's Vineyard*.Cambridge: Harvard University Press [2003].

Gross, Richard H., et al. 1983. "Early Management and Decision Making for the Treatment of Myelomeningocele." *Pediatrics* 72, 4 (October).

Grubbs v. Barbourville Family Health Center. 2003. 120 S.W.3d 682, 689, S.C.Ky.

Hall, Kim, Q. 2002. "Feminism, Disability and Embodiment." NWSA *Journal* 14, 3 (Fall).

Harder, Henry G., and Liz R. Scott. 2005. *Comprehensive Disability Management*. Philadelphia: Elsevier Science.

Harmon, Amy. 2004. "Burden of Knowledge: Tracking Parental Health; In New Tests for Fetal Defects, Agonizing Choices for Parents." *New York Times,* June 30. <www.nytimes.com/2004/06/20/us/burden-knowledge-tracking-prenatal-health-new-tests-for-fetal-defects-agonizing.html?src=pm>.

Harris, Barbara. 2009. "End of Year Letter 2009: From Barbara Harris, Founder and Executive Director." Project Prevention. <projectprevention.org/whats-new/>.

Hassed, Susan J., Connie H. Miller, Sandra K Pope, Pamela Murphy, Gerald J. Quirk Jr. and Christopher Cunniff. 1993. "Perinatal Lethal Conditions: The Effect of Diagnosis on Decision Making." *Obstetrics & Gynecology* 82, 1 (July).

Health Law Litigation Reporter. 2003. "Fertility Clinic to Face Medical Malpractice Claim." *Health Law Litigation Reporter* 10, 12.

Help Me Find A Cure. n.d. "Multiple Sclerosis Stops People from Moving." <helpmefindacure.com>.

Henry, Molly. 2007. "Do I Look Fat? Perceiving Obesity Under the *Americans with Disabilities Act*." *Ohio State Law Journal* 68, 6.

Herndon, April. 2002. "Disparate but Disabled: Fat Embodiment and Disability Studies" NWSA *Journal* 14, 3 (Autumn).

Hershey, Laura. 1993. "Wade Blank's Liberated Community." In Barrett Shaw (ed.), *The Ragged Edge: The Disability Experience from the Pages of the First Fifteen Years of the Disability Rag*. Louisville: Avocado Press [1994].

Hitler, Adolf. 1939. *Mein Kampf*. New York: Hurst and Blackett.

Hoag, Hannah. 2008. "Inducing Seizures Among Seniors." *Canadian Medical Association Journal* 178, 10 (May).

Holmes, M. Morgan. 2008. "Mind the Gaps: Intersex and (Re-productive) Spaces in Disability Studies and Bioethics." *Journal of Bioethical Inquiry* 5, 2–3.

Horsburgh et al. 2009. "A Behavioural Genetic Study on Mental Toughness and Personality." *Personality and Individual Difference* 46, 2 (January).

Hubbard, Ruth. 1990a. "Abortion and Disability: Who Should and Should Not Inhabit the World?" In Lennard J. Davis (ed.), *The Disability Studies Reader*. 3rd ed. New York: Routledge [2010].

_____. 1990b. *The Politics of Wopmen's Biology*. New Brunswick: Rutgers University Press.

Hubbard, Ruth, and Elijah Wald. 1993. *Exploding the Gene Myth*. Boston: Beacon Press.

Huizinga, Mary Margaret, Lisa A. Cooper, Sara N. Bleich, Jeanne M. Clark and Mary Catherine Beach. 2009. "Physician Respect for Patients with Obesity." *Journal of General Internal Medicine* 24, 11.

Human Resources and Skills Development Canada. 2007. "Chapter 7: Aboriginal People with Disabilities." *Advancing the Inclusion of People with Disabilities 007.* <http://www.rhdcc-hrsdc.gc.ca/eng/disability_issues/reports/fdr/2007/page09.shtml>.

Huntington Society of Canada. n.d. "Public Service Announcement (PSA) Campaign." <huntingtonsociety.ca/english/content/?page=Ad%20Campaign>.

Immigration and Refugee Protection Act S.C. 2001 Chapter 27.

Income Support Advocacy Centre. 2010. "Fact Sheet: Social Assistance Rates." Link off of main page at: <incomesecurity.org>.

Independent Living Canada. n.d. "IL Centres Across Canada." <ilcanada.ca/article/il-centres-across-canada-166.asp>.

Izzard v. Cosmopolitan Industries Ltd. 2002 SKQB 200.

Jaeger, Paul T., and Cynthia Ann Bowman. 2005. *Understanding Disability: Inclusion, Access, Diversity, and Civil Rights*. Westport, CT: Praeger Publishers.

Jarrett, Mary. 1921. "Psychiatric Social Work." *Proceedings of the National Conference of Social Work, Milwaukee, Wisconsin*. Chicago: University of Chicago Press.

Johnson, Harriet. "Frequently Asked Questions about the Telethon Protest." *Crip Commentary*. <cripcommentary.com/faq.html>.

Jutel, Annemarie. 2011. "Classification, Disease and Diagnosis." *Perspectives in Biology and Medicine* 54, 2 (Spring).

Kallianes, Virginia, and Phyllis Rubenfeld. 1997. "Disabled Women and Reproductive Rights." *Disability and Society* 12, 2.

Kameny, Frank. 2009. "How It All Started." *Journal of Gay & Lesbian Mental Health* 13, 2.

_____. 1965. "Civil Liberties: A Progress Report." *New York Mattachine Newsletter* (July). <rainbowhistory.org/kameny75b.pdf>.

Keel v. Banach. 1993. Supreme Court of Alabama. 624 So. 2D 1022.

Kessler, Suzanne J. 1998. *Lessons from the Intersexed*. Brunswick: Rutgers University Press.

Kevles, Daniel J. 2000. "The Ghost of Galton: Eugenics Past, Present and Future." In Michael Alan Signer (ed.), *Humanity at the Limit: The Impact of the Holocaust*

Experience on Jews and Christians. Bloomington: Indiana University Press.

____. 1985. *In the Name of Eugenics: Genetics and the Uses of Human Heredity*. Berkeley: University of California Press [1986].

Kimmelman, Barbara. 1983. "The American Breeders' Association: Genetics and Eugenics in an Agricultural Context, 1903–13." *Social Studies of Science* 13, 2 (May).

King, Samantha. 2001. "An All-Consuming Cause: Breast Cancer, Corporate Philanthropy and the Market for Generosity." *Social Text* 19, 4 (Winter).

Kirec v. Canada (Minister of Citizenship & Immigration). 2006. FC 800.

Kissack, Terence. 1995. "Freaking Fag Revolutionaries: New York's Gay Liberation Front, 1969–1971." *Radical History Review* 62, 2 (Spring).

Klein, Naomi. 2007. *The Shock Doctrine: The Rise of Disaster Capitalism*. Toronto: Alfred A. Knopf Canada.

Kline, Wendy. 2001. *Building A Better Race: Gender Sexuality, and Eugenics from the Turn of the Century to the Baby Boom*. Berkley: University of California Press.

Kolb, Lawrence C. 1953 "Clinical Evaluation of Prefrontal Lobotomy." *JAMA* 152, 12 (July).

Lane, Harlan. 2008. "Do Deaf People Have a Disability?" In H. Dirksen and L. Bauman (eds.), *Open Your Eyes: Deaf Studies Talking*. Minneapolis: University of Minnesota Press.

____. 1995. "Construction of Deafness." In Lennard J. Davis (ed.), *The Disability Studies Reader*. 3rd ed. New York: Routleddge [2010].

Lane, Harlan, Robert Hoffmeister and Ben Bahan. 1996. *A Journey into the Deaf-World*. San Diego: Dawnsign Press.

Lavender, Harold. 2003. "Campaigning Against Cutbacks to People with Disabilities." *New Socialist* 39 (Dec.–Jan.)

Lemons, J. Stanley. 1990. *The Woman Citizen: Social Feminism in the 1920s*. Charlottesville: University Press of Virginia.

Leonard, John W. 2009. "Note: Defining Disabled: A Study of the ADA Amendments Act of 2008 in Eliminating the Consideration of Certain Mitigating Measures." *Journal of Contemporary Health Law & Policy* 26, 1 (Fall).

Lepofsky, M. David. 2004. "The Long, Arduous Road to a Barrier-Free Ontario for People With Disabilities: History of the *Ontarians with Disabilities Act* — The First Chapter." *National Journal of Constitutional Law*. <http://www.crvawc. ca/documents/The%20History%20of%20the%20Ontarians%20with%20 Disabilities%20Act.pdf>.

Li, C.C. 2000. "Progressing from Eugenics to Human Genetics: Celebrating the 70th Birthday of Professor Newton E. Morton." *Human Heredity* 50, 1 (Jan.–Feb).

Liao, Fang-Lian. 1996. "Illegal Immigrants in Garment Sweatshops: The Universal Declaration of Human Rights and the International Covenant on Civil and Political Rights." *Southwestern Journal of Law and Trade in the Americas* 3, 2 (Fall).

Liao, S. Matthew, Julian Savulescu and Mark Sheehan. 2007. "The Ashley Treatment: Best Interests, Convenience, and Parental Decision-Making." *The Hastings Center Report* 37, 2 (Mar.–Apr.).

Liddington, et al. v. Burns et al., US District Court for the Western District of Oklahoma,

October 31.

Lifton, Robert Jay. 1986. *The Nazi Doctors: Medical Killing and the Psychology of Genocide*. New York, Basic Books.

Linton, Simi. 1998. *Claiming Disability: Knowledge and Identity*. New York: New York University Press.

Little, Sarah E., Vanitha Janakiraman, Anjali Kaimal, Thomas Musci, Jeffrey Ecker, and Aaron B. Caughey. 2010. "The Cost-Effectivenss of Prenatal Screening for Spinal Muscular Atrophy." *American Journal of Obstetrics and Gynecology* 202, 3 (March).

Liu, Shiliang, K.S. Joseph, Michael S. Kramer, Alexander C. Allen, Reg Sauve, I.D. Rusen and Shi Wu Wen. 2002. "Relationship of Prenatal Diagnosis and Pregnancy Termination to Overall Infant Mortality in Canada." *JAMA* 287, 12.

Longmore, Paul K. 2005. "The Hand That Feeds… Charity Telethons & Disability Activism." Ryerson University, November 11. <ryecast.ryerson.ca/dmpstreams/rbc2005/index.asp>.

____. 2003. *Why I Burned My Book and Other Essays on Disability*. Philadelphia: Temple University Press.

Luther, Emily. 2010. "Justice for All Shapes and Sizes: Combating Discrimination in Canada." *Alberta Law Review* 48, 1.

Mahwald, Mary Briody. 2000. *Genes, Women, Equality*. New York: Oxford University Press.

Maine, Margo. 2000. *Body Wars: Making Peace with Women's Bodies: An Activist' Guide*. Carlsbad, CA: Gürze Books.

Malthus, Thomas. 1888. *An Essay on the Principle of Population: Or, A View of Its Past and Present Effects on Human Happiness*. 9th ed. London: Reeves and Turner.

Mansfield, Caroline, Suellen Hopfler and Theresa M. Marteau. 1999. "Termination Rates After Prenatal Diagnosis of Down Syndrome, Spina Bifida, Anencephaly, and Turner and Klinefelter Syndromes: A Systematic Literature Review." *Prenatal Diagnosis* 19, 9 (September).

Manuel, Frank E. 1992. "A Requiem for Karl Marx." *Daedalus* 121, 2 (Spring).

March of Dimes Foundation. 2010. *Working Together for Stronger, Healthier Babies: March of Dimes Annual Report 2010*. <marchofdimes.com/downloads/2010_Annual_Report.pdf>.

____. 2007. "Don't You Dare." <www.phac-aspc.gc.ca/fa-af/fa-af08-eng.php>.

____. n.d. *Pregnancy & Overweight, Obese Women*. <www.marchofdimes.com/39679_55530.asp>.

Marchand, Roland. 1985. *Advertising the American Dream: Making Way for Modernity, 1920–1940*. Berkeley: University of California Press [1986].

Marcovitch, Harvey. 2010. *Black's Medical Dictionary*. 42nd ed. London: A & C Black Publishers.

Marcus, Eric. 1992. *Making History: The Struggle for Gay and Lesbian Equal Rights 1945–1990: An Oral History*. New York: Harper Collins.

Marks, Deborah. 1999. *Disability: Controversial Debates and Psychosocial Perspectives*. London: Routledge.

Marx, Karl. 1875. *Critique of the Gotha Programme*. New York: International Publishers

[1938].

Matthews, Gerald, Ian J. Deary and Martha C. Whiteman. 2003. *Personality Traits*. 2nd ed. Cambridge: Press Syndicate of the University of Cambridge.

May, Elaine Tyler. 1995. *Barren in the Promised Land: Childless Americans and the Pursuit of Happiness*. Cambridge: Harvard University Press [1997].

McCabe, Martina P., and Loraine Leas. 2008. "A Qualitative Study of Primary Health Care Access, Barriers and Satisfaction Among People with Mental Illness." *Psychology, Health & Medicine* 13, 3 (May).

McKay-Panos v. Air Canada. 2006. F.C.J. No. 28

McNeill, Paul Murray. 1993. *The Ethics and Politics of Human Experimentation*. Cambridge: Cambridge University Press.

McRuer, Robert. 2006 *Crip Theory: Cultural Signs of Queerness and Disability*. New York: New York University Press.

____. 2003a. "Critical Investments: AIDS, Christopher Reeve, and Queer/Disability Studies." *Journal of Medical Humanities* 20, 3/4 (Winter).

____. 2003b. "As Good as it Gets: Queer Theory and Critical Disability." GLQ: *A Journal of Lesbian and Gay Studies* 9, 1/2.

____. 2002. "Compulsory Able-Bodiedness and Queer/Disabled Existence." In Sharon L. Snyder, Brenda Jo Brueggemann and Rosemarie Garland-Thomson (eds.), *Disability Studies: Enabling the Humanities*. New York: Modern Language Association of America.

Medline Plus. n.d. "Cystic Fibrosis." <nlm.nih.gov/medlineplus/ency/article/000107>.

Miller, Adam. 1994–1995. "The Pioneer Fund: Bankrolling the Professors of Hate." *The Journal of Blacks in Higher Education* 6 (Winter).

Miller, Paul, Sophia Parker and Sarah Gillinson. 2004. *Disablism: How to Tackle the Last Prejudice*. London: Demos.

Mingus, Mia. 2011. "Moving Toward the Ugly: A Politic Beyond Desirability." *Femmes of Color Symposium Keynote Speech*. August 21. <leavingevidence.wordpress. com/2011/08/22/moving-toward-the-ugly-a-politic-beyond-desirability/>.

Ministry of Community and Social Services. 2010. *Income of Social Assistance Recipients*. <mcss.gov.on.ca/en/mcss/publications/social/sarac/recipients_sarac.aspx on>.

Minnesota Historical Society. n.d. "Minnesota Eugenics Society & Founder Charles Fremont Dight." <www.mnhs.org/library/tips/history_topics/117eugenics. html>.

Moalen, Sharon, and Jonathan Price. 2007. *Survival of the Sickest: A Medical Maverick Discovers Why We Need Disease*. New York: William Morrow.

Moore, Leroy. 2002. "Disabled People of Colour: Oppression is the Womb of Self-Determination." Ryerson University International Day for the Elimination of Racial Discrimination. Toronto, March 21.

Morris, Jenny. 2001. "Impairment and Disability: Constructing an Ethics of Care that Promotes Human Rights." *Hypatia* 16, 4 (Fall).

____. 1991. *Pride Against Prejudice: Transforming Attitudes to Disability*. Philadelphia: New Society Publishers.

Mosby's Medical Dictionary. 2006. 7th edition. St. Louis: Mosby's.

Muhammad, Lawrence. 1999. "Philip Morris Cos. in a Hunger Fight." USA *Today* March 11.

Muir v. Alberta. 1996, 132 D.L.R. (4th) 695 (AB. Crt. Q.B.).

Musci, Thomas J., and Aaron B. Caughey. 2005. "Cost-effectiveness Analysis of Prenatal Population-based Fragile X Carrier Screening" *American Journal of Obstetrics and Gynecology* 192, 6 (June).

Muscular Dystrophy Association. 2009a. *2009 Annual Report.* <mda.org/special/ annual/2009AnnualReport.pdf>.

____. 2009b "Tax Form 990." <mda.org/special/taxforms/2009-990FederalReturn. pdf>.

____. 2006. "Help Fight Muscular Dystrophy One Shamrock at a Time." <mda.org/ news/060301shamrocks>.

Muscular Dystrophy Canada. 2009–2010. *Walk With Champions: 2009–2010 Annual Report.* <www.muscle.ca/fileadmin/National/About_Us/Annual_ Report/2010_E.pdf>.

National Alliance for Research on Schizophrenia and Depression. 2010. *Combined Financial Statements and Supplemental Material.* <narsad.org/userFiles/2010_ Combined_Financial_Statements.pdf>.

National Disability Rights Network. 2011. *Segregated and Exploited: The Failure of the Disability Service System to Provide Quality Work.* Washington, DC. <www. napas.org/images/Documents/Resources/Publications/Reports/Segregated- and-Exploited.pdf>.

National Centre for Biotechnology Information. n.d.a. "Search Result for Clinic Location(s): United States." <http://www.ncbi.nlm.nih.gov/sites/GeneTests/ clinic/location/?db=genetests&country=United%20States>.

____. n.d.b. "Search Result for Laboratory Location(s): United States." <http://www. ncbi.nlm.nih.gov/sites/GeneTests/lab/location/?db=genetests&country=Uni ted%20States>.

Nelson, Jack A. 2003. "The Invisible Cultural Group: Images of Disability." In Paul M. Lester and Susan D. Ross (eds.), *Images That Injure: Pictorial Stereotypes in the Media.* 2nd ed. Westport, CT: Praeger Publishers.

New Internaitonalist. 2005. "Disability in the Majority World: The Facts." *New Internationalist* 384 (November).

Newbeck, Phyl. 2004. *Virginia Hasn't Always Been for Lovers: Interracial Marriage Bans and the Case of Richard and Mildred Loving.* Carbondale: Southern Illinois University Press.

Nind, Naomi A. 2000. "Solving an Appalling Problem: Social Reformers and the Campaign for the Alberta Sexual Sterilization Act, 1928." *Alberta Law Review* 38, 2 (August).

Nixon, Ron. 2008. "Fighting AIDS — by Going Shopping; Red Raises $14 Million, But Critics Object to the Mix." *The International Herald Tribune,* February 6.

No Force Coalition. 2000. *Electroshock Fact Sheet: Mental Health Issues Primer.* 3.

Nursing Standard. 2006. "I Was Made to Go Without Food." *Nursing Standard* 20, 44.

O'Neil, Sandy. 2001. *First they Killed The 'Crazies' and the 'Cripples': The Ableist*

Persecution and Murders of People with Disabilities by Nazi Germany 1933–45, An Anthropological Perspective. Ann Arbor, MI: UMI Dissertation Services.

O'Toole, Marie T. (ed.). 2003. *Miller-Keane Encyclopedia and Dictionary of Medicine, Nursing and Applied Health*. 7th edition. Philadelphia: Saunders.

OECD. 2010. *Sickness, Disability and Work: Breaking the Barriers: Canada: Opportunits for Collaboration*. <www.oecd.org/dataoecd/16/13/46093870.pdf>.

Oliver, Mike. 2009. *Understanding Disability: from Theory to Practice*. Houndmills: Palgrave MacMillan.

____. 2004. "The Social Model in Action: If I had a Hammer." In Colin Barnes and Geof Mercer (eds.), *Implementing the Social Model of Disability: Theory and Research*. Leeds: The Disability Press.

____. 1996. *Understanding Disability: from Theory to Practice*. New York: St. Martin's Press.

____. 1990 *The Politics of Disablement*. Houndmills: Macmillan Press.

Olsen, Douglas G., John W. Pracejus and Norman R. Brown. 2003. "When Profit Equals Price: Consumer Confusion about Donation Amounts in Cause-Related Marketing." *Journal of Public Policy & Marketing* 22, 2 (Fall).

Ontario. 2010. "People and Culture — Population Densities." <Ontario.ca/en/about_ontario/EC001035>.

Ontario Disability Support Program Act (ODSPA) (1997: 4. (1)(b))

Ontario Disability Support Program Act. S.O. 1997, Chapter 25. Schedule B.

Ontario March of Dimes. 2009–2010. *Ontario March of Dimes Annual Report 2009–2010*: See *the Forest Not Just the Tree*. <www.marchofdimes.ca/EN/AboutUs/Documents/Annual%20Reports/Omod_AR_2010.pdf>.

____. 2008–2009. *One Stop: Solutions for Independence: 2008–2009 Annual Report*. <www.marchofdimes.ca/EN/AboutUs/Documents/Annual%20Reports/2009_AR.pdf>.

Ontario's *Occupational Health and Safety Act*. R.S.O. 1990, C. O.1

Ordover, Nancy. 2003. *American Eugenics: Race, Queer Anatomy, and the Science of Nationalism*. Minneapolis: University of Minnesota Press.

Osborn, Frederick. 1968. *The Future of Human Heredity: An Introduction to Eugenics in Modern Society*. New York: Weybright & Talley.

Ottawa Citizen. 1985. "JP Rules Safety Act Doesn't Cover Disabled Workshop." *Ottawa Citizen*, October 8.

Paola, Frederick Adolf, Robert Walker and Lois LaCivita Nixon. 2010. *Medical Ethics and Humanities*. Mississauga: Jones and Bartlett Publishers.

Parens, Erik and Adrienne Asch. 1999. "Special Supplement: The Disability Rights Critique of Prenatal Genetic Testing Reflections and Recommendations." *Hastings Center Report* 29, 5.

Parens, Penny, Debra Cameron, Nancy Christie, Lynn Cockburn, Goli Hashemi and Karen Yoshida. 2009. "Disability in Low-Income Countries: Issues and Implications." *Disability and Rehabilitation* 31, 14.

Paul, Diane B. 1985. "Commentary: Textbook Treatments of the Genetics of Intelligence." *The Quarterly Review of Biology* 60, 3 (September).

People First of Canada. 2006. "About Us." <http://www.peoplefirstofcanada.ca/about_us_en.php>.

Peters, Yvonne. 2003. "From Charity to Equality: Canadians with Disabilities Take Their Rightful Place in Canada's Constitution." In Deborah Stienstra and Aileen Wight-Felske (eds.), *Making Equality: History of Advocacy and People with Disabilities in Canada*. Concord, ON: Captus Press.

Petersen, Amy. 2006. "An African-American Woman with Disabilities: The Intersection of Gender Race and Disability." *Disability and Society 21, 7*.

Pfeiffer, David. 2003. "The Disability Studies Paradigm." In Patrick Devlieger, Frank Rusch and David Pfeiffer (eds.), *Rethinking Disability: The Emergence of New Definitions, Concepts and Communities*. Antwerpen: Garant [2007].

____. 1993. "Overview of the Disability Movement: History, Legislative Record and Political Implications." *Policy Studies Journal 21, 4*.

Phillips, Cassandra. 2001. "Re-imagining the (Dis)Abled Body." *Journal of Medical Humanities 22, 3* (September).

Pioneer Fund. n.d.a "About Us." <pioneerfund.org>.

____. n.d.b. "Grantees." <pioneerfund.org/Grantees.html>.

Pollanen, Michael S., David A. Chiasson, James T. Cairns, and James G. Young. 1998. "Unexpected Death Related to Restraint for Excited Delirium: A Retrospective Study of Deaths in Police Custody and in the Community." *Canadian Medical Association Journal 158, 12* (June.)

Pracejus, John W., and G. Douglas Olsen. 2004. "The Role of Brand/Cause Fit in the Effectiveness of Cause-Related Marketing Campaigns." *Journal of Business Research 57, 6* (June).

Prada, Paulo, and Andy Pasztor. 2008. "American Airlines Hit by $7.1 Million in Fines." *The Wall Street Journal* August 15.

Preece, Julia. 1996. "Class and Disability: Influences on Learning Expectations." *Disability and Society 11, 2*.

Prentice, Alison L. 1988. *Canadian Women: A History*. San Diego: Harcourt Brace Jovanovich.

Proctor, Robert N. 2002. "Eugenics in Hitler's Germany." In Donna F. Ryan and John S. Schuchman (eds.), *Deaf People in Hitler's Europe*. Washington DC:, Gallaudet University Press.

Project Prevention. 2011. "Statistics." At: <projectprevention.org/statistics>.

____. 1999. "Sad Reality." <projectprevention.org/the-sad-reality>.

____. n.d. <projectprevention.org>.

Province, William B. 1973. "Geneticists and the Biology of Race Crossing." *Science 182, 4114* (November).

Public Health Agency of Canada. 2008. "Folic Acid and Prevention of Neural Tube Defects: Information Update from PHAC — 2008." <www.phac-aspc.gc.ca/fa-af/fa-af08-eng.php>.

Quebec (Commision des droits de la personne et des droits de la jeunesse) v. Montreal (City); Quebec (Commission des droits de la personne et des droits de la jeunesse) v. Boisbriand (City), 2000 SCC 27.

Quirks and Quarks. 2008. "Shock Therapy." With Bob McDonald. CBC Radio One. October 7. <cbc.ca/quirks/episode/2008/03/08/shock-therapy-white-shark-cafe-battling-loons-wolves-and-cyotes-make-your-own-event-horizon/>.

____. 2006. "Rethinking Autism." With Bob McDonald. Prod. by Motluk, Alison. CBC Radio One. October 7. <cbc.ca/quirks/episode/2006/10/07/nobel-prize-for-physics-nobel-prize-for-physiology-or-medicine-a-whale-of-an-imitation-rethinking-au/>.

Rabino, Isaac 2003. "Genetic Testing and Its Implications: Human Genetics Researchers Grapple with Ethical Issues." *Science, Technology and Human Values* 28, 3 (Summer).

Raphael, Dennis. 2007. *Poverty and Policy in Canada: Implications for Health and Quality of Life.* Toronto: Canadian Scholars' Press.

Read, John, and Richard Bentall. 2010. "The Effectiveness of Electroconvulsive Therapy: A Literature Review." *Epidemiologia e Psichiatria Sociale* 19, 4 (Oct.–Dec.).

Rees, Laurence. 2005. *Auschwitz: A New History.* New York: Public Affairs.

Reeve, Christopher. 1998. *Still Me.* New York: Random House.

Reeve, Donna. 2004. "Psycho-Emotional Dimensions of Disability and the Social Model." In Colin Barnes and Geof Mercer (eds.), *Implementing the Social Model of Disability: Theory and Research.* Leeds: Disability Press.

Rehabilitation Act of 1973, 29 U.S.C. § 794 (and amendments).

Rentoul, Robert Reid. 1906. *Race Culture or Race Suicide: A Plea for the Unborn.* New York: Garland Publishing [1984].

Reverby, Susan. 2009. *Examining Tuskegee: The Infamous Syphilis Study and its Legacy.* Chapel Hill: University of North Carolina Press.

Rick Hansen Foundation. n.d. "Man In Motion World Tour Overview." <rickhansen.com/code/navigate.aspx?Id=17>.

Riessman, Catherine Kohler. 1998. "Women and Medicalization: A New Perspective." In Gill Kirkup and Laurie S. Keller (eds.), *Inventing Women: Science, Technology, and Gender.* Malden, MA: Blackwell Publishers.

Rimmerman, Craig A. 2008. *The Lesbian and Gay Movements: Assimilation or Liberation.* Boulder: Westview Press.

Roberts, Dorothy. 1997. *Killing the Black Body: Race, Reproduction, and the Meaning of Liberty.* New York: Pantheon Books.

Roberts, Wayne. 1979. "'Rocking the Cradle for the World': The New Woman and Maternal Feminism, Toronto, 1877–1914." *A Not Unreasonable Claim: Women and Reform in Canada, 1880s–1920s.* Toronto: Women's Educational Press.

Robertson, Gerald. 1996. "Appendix A." *Muir v. Alberta,* 132 D.L.R. (4th) 695 (AB. Crt. Q.B.), (Lexis 1056).

Robitsche, Jonas B. 1973. *Eugenic Sterilization.* Springfield: Charles C. Thomas.

Rohrer, Judy. 2005, "Toward a Full-Inclusion Feminism: A Feminist Employment of Disability Analysis." *Feminist Studies* 31, 1 (Spring).

Rosano, Aldo, Federica Mancini and Alessandro solipacia. 2008. "Poverty in People with Disabilities: Indicators from the Capability Approach." *Social Indicators Research* 94, 1 (October).

Rowen, Lisa. 2008. "Weight Stigmatization and Bias." *Bariatric Nursing and Surgical Patient Care* 3, 1 (March).

Rowen, Tami. 2006. "What Can Disability Studies Contribute to the Treatment of People with Obesity?" *Bariatric Nursing and Surgical Patient Care* 1, 3 (Fall).

Rowland, Robyn. 1992. *Living Labrotories: Women and Reproductive Technologies*. Bloomington, IN: Indiana University Press.

Rucker, Patrick, and Jonathan Stempel. 2009. "Bank of America Gets Big Government Bailout." *Reuters,* January 16. <www.reuters.com/article/idUS-TRE50F1Q720090116>.

Rushton, J. Philippe. 1995. *Race, Evolution, and Behavior*. New Brunswick, NJ: Transaction.

Rushton, J. Philippe, and Arthur R. Jensen. 2010. "The Rise and Fall of the Flynn Effect as a Reason to Expect a Narrowing of the Black–White IQ Gap." *Intelligence* 38, 2 (March).

Russell, Marta. 2002. "What Disability Civil Rights Cannot Do: Employment and Political Economy." *Disability & Society* 17, 2.

Saigal, Saroj, et al. 1999. "Differences in Preferences for Neonatal Outcomes Among Health Care Professionals, Parents, and Adolescents." *JAMA* 281, 21 (June 2).

Sandahl, Carrie. 2003. "Queering the Crip or Cripping the Queer? Intersections of Queer and Crip Identities in Solo Autobiographical Performance." *GLQ* 9, 1–2.

Sanger, Margaret. 1925. "Introduction." In Margaret Sanger (ed.), *International Aspects of Birth Control, The Sixth International Neo-Malthusian and Birth Control Conference, Volume 1*. New York: American Birth Control League.

Schechtman, Kenneth B., Diana l. Gray, Jack D. Baty and Steven Rothman. 2002. "Decision Making for Termination of Pregnancies with Fetal Anomalies: Analysis of 53,000 Pregnancies." Obstetrics & Gynecology 99, 2 (February).

Schizophrenia Society of Canada. 2008–2009. *Annual Report*. <schizophrenia.ca/sscAnnualReport0809.pdf>.

Settlement.org. 2008–2009. "How Much Does it Cost to Rent an Apartment in Ontario?" <settlement.org/sys/faqs_detail.asp?k=RENT_BASIC&faq_id=4001280>.

Shaffer, Brian L., Aaron B. Caughey and Mary E. Norton. 2006. "Variation in the Decision to Terminate Pregnancy in the Setting of Fetal Aneuploidy." *Prenatal Diagnosis* 26, 8 (August).

Shakespeare, Tom. 2006a. "The Social Model of Disability." In Lennard J. Davis (ed.), *The Disability Studies Reader*. 3rd ed. New York: Routledge [2010].

____. 2006b. *Disability Rights and Wrongs*. London: Routledge.

____. 1998. "Choices and Rights: Eugenics, Genetics and Disability Equality." *Disability and Society* 13, 5 (November).

Shakespeare, Tom, and Nicholas Watson. 2001. "The Social Model of Disability: An Outdated Ideology?" In Sharon Barnartt and Barbara Altman (eds.), *Exploring Theories and Expanding Methodologies: Research in Social Science and Disability*. Vol. 2. Stamford, CT: JAI Press.

Sharma v. Canada (Citizenship and Immigration). 2010. FC 398.

Shapiro, Joseph P. 1993. *No Pity: People with Disabilities Forging a New Civil Rights*

Movement. New York: Times Books [1994].

Shaw, Anthony. 1988. "QL Revised." *The Hastings Centre Report* 18, 2 (April-May).

Sherry, Mark. 2007. "(Post)Colonizing Disability." In Lennard J. Davis (ed.), *The Disability Studies Reader.* New York: Routledge [2010].

____. 2004. "Overlaps and Contradicitons Between Queer Theory and Disability Studies." *Disability and Society* 19, 7.

Shildrick, Margrit. 2009. *Dangerous Discourses of Disabiltiy, Subjectivity and Sexuality.* Houndmills: Palgrave Macmillan.

Shildrick, Margrit, and Janet Price. 1998. "Uncertain Thoughts on the Dis/abled Body." In Margrit Shildrick and Janet Price (eds.), *Vital Signs: Feminist Reconfigurations of the Bio/logical Body.* Edinburgh: University Press.

Shorter, Edward. 1997. *History of Psychiatry: From the Era of the Asylum to the Age of Prozac.* New York: John Wiley & Sons.

Silberman, Steve. 2010. "Exclusive: First Autistic Presidential Appointee Speaks Out." *Wired* October 6. <wired.com/wiredscience/2010/10/exclusive-ari-neeman-qa/all/1>.

Silver, Michael G. 2003–2004. "Eugenics and Compulsory Sterilization Laws: Providing Redress for the Victims of a Shameful Era in United States History Note." *George Washington Law Review* 72, 4 (April).

Silverstein, Charles. 2008. "Are You Saying Homosexuality Is Normal?" *Journal of Gay & Lesbian Mental Health*, 12, 3.

Sinnott, Edmund, and Leslie Dunn. 1925. *Principles of Genetics: An Elementary Text, with Problems.* New York: McGraw-Hill.

Smith, David. 2009. *Ignored, Shunned, and Invisible: How the Label "Retarded" Has Denied Freedom and Dignity to Millions.* Westport: Greenwood.

Smith, Steven R. 2005. "Equality, Identity and the Disability Rights Movement: From Policy to Practice and from Kant to Nietzsche in More than One Uneasy Move." *Critical Social Policy* 25, 4 (November).

Snow, Kattie. 2010. "To Ensure Inclusion, Freedom, and Respect for All, It's Time to Embrace People First Language." <www.disabilityisnatural.com/images/PDF/pfl09.pdf>.

Social Benefits Tribunal. 2008–2009. "Tribunal ODSP Decisions by Issue and Outcome: 2008–2009." *Annual Report2008-2009.* <sbt.gov.on.ca/AssetFactory.aspx?did=125>.

Social Security Online. 2010. "What Are the Categories of Eligibility?" *Social Security Handbook* [2112]. <www.socialsecurity.gov/OP_Home/handbook/handbook.21/handbook-2112.html>.

Somerville, Margaret. 2011. "'Deselecting' our Children." *Globe and Mail,* August 22.

Sorrell, Justin C. 2010. "Rehabilitative Employees and the National Labor Relations Act." *William and Mary Law Review* 52, 2 (November).

Spallone, Patricia. 1989. *Beyond Conception: The New Politics of Reproduction.* Massachusetts: Bergin and Garvey Publishers.

State Div. of Human Rights ex rel. McDermott v. Xerox Corp. 1985. Court of Appeals of New York, 65 N.Y.2d 213

Stewart, Jean, and Marta Russell. 2001. "Disablement, Prison and Historical Segregation." *Monthly Review* 53, 3 (July August).

Stienstra, Deborah, and Aileen Wight-Felske. 2003. "Introduction: Making Equality and History." In *Making Equality: History of Advocacy and Persons with Disabilities in Canada.* Concord, ON: Captus Press.

Stiker, Henri-Jacques.1999. In William Sayers (trans), *A History of Disability.* Ann Arbor: University of Michigan Press [2009].

Stole, Inger L. 2008. "Philanthropy as Public Relations: A Critical Perspective on Cause Marketing." *International Journal of Commutation* 2.

Strahilevitz, Michal. 1999. "The Effects of Product Type and Donation Magnitude on Willingness to Pay More for Charity-Linked Brand." *Journal of Consumer Psychology* 8, 3.

Stroman, Duane F. 2003. *The Disability Rights Movement: From Deinstitutionalization to Self-Determination.* Lanham, Maryland: University Press of America.

Stuart, O.W. 1992. "Race and Disability: Just a Double Oppression?" In Len Barton (ed.), *Overcoming Disabling Barriers: 18 Years of Disability & Society.* New York: Routledge [2006].

Stubblefield, Anna. 2009. "Race, Disability, and the Social Contract." *The Southern Journal of Philosophy* 47, S1 (Spring).

Sullivan, Laura. 2007. "Death by Excited Delirium, Diagnosis or Coverup?" National Public Radio. February 26. <npr.org/templates/story/story. php?storyId=7608386>.

Summers, Lawrence H. 2005. "Remarks at the NBER Conference on Diversifying the Science & Engineering Workforce." *National Bureau of Economic Research* Conference, Cambridge, January 14. <isites.harvard.edu/fs/docs/icb. topic469725.files/Remarks%20at%20NBER%20Conference%20on%20 Diversifying%20the%20Science.pdf>.

Swain, John, and Sally French. 2000. "Towards an Affirmation Model of Disability." *Disability & Society* 15,4.

Szasz, Thomas Stephen. 2007. *Coercion as Cure: A Critical History of Psychiatry.* New Brunswick: Transaction Publishers.

Tait, Janice J. 1985–86. "Reproductive Technology and the Rights of Disabled Persons." *Canadian Journal of Women and the Law* 1.

Taylor v. Kurapati. 1999. N.W.2d 670, Mich. C.A.

Taylor, Steven. 2002. "Disabled Workers Deserve Real Choices, Real Jobs." <www. accessiblesociety.org/topics/economics-employment/shelteredwksps.html>

Terry, Jennifer. 1995. "Anxious Slippages Between 'Us' and 'Them.'" In Jennifer Terry and Jacqueline L. Urla (eds.), *Deviant Bodies: Critical Perspectives on Difference in Science and Poplar Culture (Race, Gender, and Science).* Bloomington: Indiana University Press.

Tervo, Raymond C., Scot Azuma, Glen Palmer and Pat Redinius. 2002. "Medical Students' Attitudes Toward Persons With Disability: A Comparative Study." *Archives of Physical Medicine and Rehabilitation* 83, 11 (November).

Thom, Deborah, and Mary Jennings. 1996. "Human Pedigree and the 'Best Stock':

from Eugenics to Genetics?" In Theresa Marteau and Martin Richards (eds.), *The Troubled Helix: Social and Psychosocial Implication of the New Human Genetics.* Cambridge: Cambridge University Press.

Thomas, Carol. 2004a. "Developing the Social Relational in the Social Model of Disability: A Theoretical Agenda." In Colin Barnes and Geof Mercer (eds.), *Implementing the Social Model of Disability: Theory and Research.* Leeds: Disability Press.

____. 2004b. "How Is Disability Understood? An Examination of Sociological Approaches." *Disability & Society* 19, 6 (October).

____. 1999. *Female Forms: Experiencing and Understanding Disability.* Buckingham: Open University Press.

Thornhill, Randy, and Craig T. Palmer. 2000. *A Natural History of Rape: Biological Bases of Sexual Coercion.* Springfield: MIT Press.

Titchkosky, Tanya. 2003. "Governing Embodiment: Technologies of Constituting Citizens with Disabilities." *Canadian Journal of Sociology* 28, 4 (Fall).

Toughill, Kelly. 1995. "Thousands Facing Loss of Disability Benefits." *Toronto Star,* October 7.

Tregaskis, Claire. 2002. "Social Model Theory: The Story So Far." *Disability & Society* 17, 4.

Troyer, A.F., and H. Stoehr. 2003. "Willet M. Hays, Great Benefactor to Plant Breeding and the Founder of Our Association." *Journal of Heredity* 94, 6.

Turmusani, Majid. 2003. *Disabled People and Economic Needs in the Developing World: A Political Perspective from Jordan.* Burlington, VT: Ashgate Publishing.

United Steel Workers. 2010. "Sears Continues Lock Out Its Warehouse Employees After Demanding Cuts." <www.newswire.ca/en/releases/archive/April2010/12/c9673.html>.

Urdang, Laurence. 2004. *The Bantam Medical Dictionary.* 5th edition. New York: Bantam.

Van Teijlingen, Edwin R., George W. Lowis and Peter McCaffery. 2004. "General Introduction to Midwifery and the Medicalization of Childbirth: Comparative Perspectives." In Edwin R. Van Teijlingen, George W. Lowis and Peter McCaffery (eds.), *Midwifery and the Medicalization of Childbirth: Comparative Perspectives.* Hauppauge, NY: Nova Science Publishers.

Vanhala, Lisa. 2011. *Making Rights a Reality? Disabiltiy Righyts Activists and Legal Mobilization.* New York: Cambridge University Press.

Varadarajan, Rajan, and Anil Menon. 1988. "Cause-Related Marketing: A Coalignment of Marketing Strategy and Corporate Philanthropy." *The Journal of Marketing* 52, 3 (July).

Vernon, Ayesha. 1999. "The Dialectics of Multiple Identities and the Disabled People's Movement." *Disability & Society* 14, 3.

____. 1996a. "A Stranger in Many Camps: The Experiences of Disabled Black and Ethnic Minority Women." In Jenny Morris (ed.), *Encounters with Strangers: Feminism and Disability.* London: Women's Press.

____. 1996b. "Fighting Two Different Battles: Unity is Preferable to Enmity." *Disability and Society* 11, 2.

Wall, Stephen, and John Colin Partridge. 1997. "Death in the Intensive Care Nursery: Physician Practice of Withdrawing and Withholding Life Support." *Pediatrics* 99, 1 (January).

Walls, Claudia. 2006. "A Very Special Wedding." *Time,* July 24.

Watt, David C. 1998. "Lionel Penrose, F.R.S. (1898–1972) and Eugenics: Part One," *Notes and Records of the Royal Society of London*, 53, 1 (January).

Weigmann, Katrin. 2005. "The Consequence of Errors: From Memory Molecules to the Criminal Chromosome, Erroneous Conclusions Continue to Blight Scientific Research." *EMBO Reports* 6, 4.

Weissman, Robert. 2008. "The System Implodes: The 10 Worst Corporations of 2008." *Multinational Monitor* 29, 3 (Nov.–Dec.).

Weitz, Don. 1988. "25 Good Reasons to Abolish Psychiatry." In Wendy Funk (ed.), *'What Difference Does it Make?' (The Journey of a Soul Survivor)*. Cranbrook, BC: Wild Flower.

Wells, John. 1998. "Abuse Charges at Brain-injury Facility in Texas: Two Canadians Among Alleged Victims, Ontario Still Recommends Treatment There." *Hamilton Spectator*, April 4.

Wendell, S. 1996. *The Rejected Body: Feminist Philosophical Reflections on Disability*. London and New York: Routledge.

_____. 1989. "Toward a Feminist Theory of Disability." *Hypatia* 4, 2.

West End Legal Services of Ottawa. 2009. *The Real Co$t of Helping Clients Pursue ODSP Justice*. <intraspec.ca/WELS_The-Real-Cost-of-Helping-CLients-Pursue-ODSP-Justice_Mar09.pdf>.

Western Report. 1995. "Two Steps Forward, One Step Back: Unrealistic Expectations Can Hurt the Mentally Handicapped, and Society as Well (Leilani Muir Case Has Revealed the Treatment of the Mentally Handicapped in the Past)." *Western Report* 10, 27 (July 24).

Wikler, Daniel. 1999. "Can We Learn From Eugenics?" *Journal of Medical Ethics* 25, 2.

Wilcox, W. F. 1922. "Birth Rate and Natural Increase of Whites and Negroes in the United States." In Raymond Pierpoint William (ed.), *Report of the Fifth International Neo-Malthusian and Birth Control Conference*. London: Heinemann.

Wilson, James C. 2002. "Disability and the Human Genome." In Lennard J. Davis (ed.), *The Disability Studies Reader*. 3rd ed. New York: Routledge [2010].

Winegar, Melanie D. 2006. "Big Tali, Broken Promises: How Title I of the Americans with Disabilities Act Failed Disabled Workers." *Hofstra Law Review* 34, 3 (Spring).

Winston, Andrew, Bethany Butzer and Mark D. Ferris. 2004. "Constructing Difference: Heredity, Intelligence and Race in Textbooks, 1930–1970." In Andre S. Winston (ed.), *Defining Difference: Race & Racism in the History of Psychology*. Washington DC: American Psychological Association.

Withers, A.J. 2010. "Definitions and Divisions: Disability, Anti-Psychiatry and Disableism." *PsychOut: A Conference for Organizing Resistance Against Psychiatry*. OISE, University of Toronto, Toronto, May 7–8.

_____. 2007. *If I Can't Dance Is it Still My Revolution Too (Two)?* Toronto: Self published.

Wolfensberger, Wolf. 2000. "A Brief Overview of Social Role Valorization." *Mental Retardation* 38, 2 (April).

Woodhull, Victoria. 1893. "The Scientific Propagation of the Human Race; Or Humanitarian Aspects of Finance and Marriage." In Victoria C. Woodhull and Michael W. Perry, *Lady Eugenist: Feminist Eugenics in the Speeches and Writing of Victorial Woodhull*. Seattle: Inkling Books [2005].

Young, Damon A., and Ruth Quibell. 2000. "Why Rights Are Never Enough: Rights, Intellectual Disability and Understanding." *Disability & Society* 15, 5.

Zames Fleischer, Doris and Frieda Zames. 2001. *The Disability Rights Movement: From Charity to Confrontation*. Philadelphia: Temple University Press.

Zastrow, Charles, and Karen K. Kirst-Ashaman. 2010. *Understanding Human Behaviour and the Social Environment*. 8th ed. Belmont: Brooks/Cole.

Zola, Irving Kenneth. 1972. "Medicine as an Institution of Social Control: The Medicalizing of Society." In David Tuckett and Joseph M. Kaufert (eds.), *Basic Readings in Medical Sociology*. London: Tavistock Publications [1978].

Zuk, Marlene. 2007. *Riddled with Life: Friendly Worms, Ladybug Sex, and the Parasites That Make Us Who We Are*. Orlando: Harcourt.

Index

United Farm Women of Alberta 14
Union of the Physically Impaired
    Against Segregation (UPIAS) 86-89,
    95-96, 99
universal design 118

Via Rail 85

Walker, Bree 28
war 15, 22, 48, 55 n7
World War I 23
World War II 24-25, 46, 53
welfare 1, 2, 52
white people 8, 17-18, 21, 23, 29, 38,
    54, 66-69, 71-72, 78-79, 85, 89, 91-
    93, 99, 101, 104, 108, 120 n4
Woodhull, Victoria 22
women 4, 11, 14, 18, 21-24, 26, 28, 30,
    41, 44, 49-51, 54, 61, 89, 91-92, 94-
    95, 99-100, 103, 105, 107-109, 115
wrongful birth 51-52
wrongful life 46, 52

YM-WCA 73-74